THE
BOOK
AND THE
SWORD

FARRAR
STRAUS
GIROUX

ALSO BY DAVID WEISS HALIVNI

Mekorot U'mesorot
(Sources and Traditions), 5 volumes

Midrash, Mishnah, and Gemara:
The Jewish Predilection for Justified Law

Peshat and Derash:
Plain and Applied Meaning in Rabbinic Exegesis

THE
BOOK
AND THE
SWORD

*A Life of Learning
in the Shadow of Destruction*

DAVID WEISS HALIVNI

Farrar, Straus and Giroux
NEW YORK

Copyright © 1996 by David Weiss Halivni
All rights reserved

Printed in the United States of America

Designed by Abby Kagan

First edition, 1996

Library of Congress Cataloging-in-Publication Data
Halivni, David.
    The book and the sword : a life of learning in the shadow of
destruction / David Weiss Halivni. — 1st ed.
        p. cm.
    ISBN 978-0-374-53169-0
    1. Halivni, David. 2. Jews—Romania—Sighetu Marmaţiei—Biography.
3. Holocaust, Jewish (1939–1945)—Romania—Sighetu Marmaţiei—Personal
narratives. 4. Holocaust survivors—New York (State)—New York—
Biography. 5. Jewish scholars—New York (State)—New York—Biography.
I. Title.
DS135.R73H36 1996
940.53'18'094984—dc20   96-19673
                                                                    CIP

Title page photograph (from left to right): The author's Aunt Ethel; his
grandfather Rabbi Shaye Weiss; his sister Channa Yitte; the author (eleven
years old); his mother, Feige (sitting). Except for the author, they all perished
in the Holocaust.

CONTENTS

The sword and the book came down from heaven tied to each other. Said the Almighty, "If you keep what is written in this book, you will be spared this sword; if not, you will be consumed by it." (Midrash Rabbah Deuteronomy 4:2) We clung to the book, yet we were consumed by the sword.

For Thou hast delivered my soul from death, my eyes from tears, and my feet from stumbling . . .
—Psalm 116:8

It was decreed for Israel that they study words of Torah in distress, in enslavement, in wandering and in uncertainty, suffering for lack of food.
—Midrash Eliyahu Rabbah, 21

For those who walked upon the ramp of Auschwitz, the Holocaust is not over.
—A Kazetnik

THE
BOOK
AND THE
SWORD

When the sound of the closing of the door, after the first child was shoved into the crematorium, reached heaven, Michael, the most beneficent of angels, could not contain himself and angrily approached God. Michael asked, "Do You now pour out Your wrath upon children? In the past, children were indirectly caught up in the slaughter. This time they are the chief target of destruction. Have pity on the little ones, O Lord." God, piqued by Michael's insolence, shouted back at him, "I am the Lord of the Universe. If you are displeased with the way I conduct the world, I will return it to void and null." Hearing these words, Michael knew that there was to be no reversal. He had heard these words once before in connection with the Ten Martyrs. He knew their effect. He went back to his place, ashen and dejected, but could not resist looking back sheepishly at God and saw a huge tear rolling down His face, destined for the legendary cup which collects tears and which, when full, will bring the redemption of the world. Alas, to Michael's horror, instead of entering the cup the tear hit its rim, most of it spilling on the ground—and the fire of the crematorium continued to burn.

1

BEFORE
My Life in Sighet

I DO not remember when I came to Sighet for the first time to live with Grandfather. But I do remember what I was learning. I was learning *Chumash*, the Pentateuch, with Rashi's commentary, and that means I was about four years old. I lived with Grandfather, Rabbi Shaye Weiss, for more than ten years, until we were separated by Josef Mengele, in Auschwitz, when we both stood before him and he sent Grandfather to the right, to death, and me to the left, to struggle and hard labor.

Mother brought us to Sighet, a small town in northern Transylvania, Romania, after her marriage with Father broke up, after she had vainly protested Father's unorthodox means of making a livelihood—after a long time of cantankerous quarrels between them, which I remember well but was too young to understand. Later, I was told that the reason Mother brought us to Sighet was that she did not trust Father with my education. I was precocious, and Grandfather was a great Talmud scholar, while my father was not. But I do not think that this was the true reason, for at the age of four I had not shown any signs of such precociousness as would warrant the drastic move of abandoning house and family and bringing us all to Sighet.

We came to Sighet from Khust. I was not born in Khust but a few kilometers away in Kobolecka Poljana, then in Czechoslovakia, now in the Ukraine, either in 1928 or, most likely, in 1927. The confusion is due to my not having been registered at birth. I was born during the High Holy Day season and my parents waited to register me until they had more time. Thus, the Hebrew and the English dates of my birth do not coincide.

Father, called Zallel Wiederman (we went by the name of Weiss since we lived with Grandfather), followed a "wonder rabbi" by the name of Wiesel (a relative of my friend the writer Elie Wiesel). The wonder rabbi, so the story has it, suddenly began to perform miracles like healing the sick (the trademark of all miracle makers) and knowing the kosher or non-kosher status of a *mezuzah* (the piece of parchment containing scriptural passages that religious Jews attach to their doorposts) without unrolling it to see whether or not it was correctly written. Father became the rabbi's *gabai*, a kind of right-hand man, handling all his affairs. I was born in this wonder rabbi's house.

This poor rabbi, the story continues, lost his miracle-making powers just as suddenly as they had appeared, and people stopped visiting him. Father lost his livelihood and moved with the family to Khust, where I stayed for the next two or three years, until Mother brought us to live with Grandfather in Sighet. The wonder rabbi, too, left

Kobolecka Poljana—for what destination nobody knew. He disappeared from the scene and was considered dead until he appeared in Sighet a year or so before our deportation to Auschwitz. He was paralyzed and moved in a wheelchair. He asked to see me, and I came. When he saw me, he was moved to tears. Was I the last confirmation of his former miraculous powers, the last residue of his glorious days, or did his tears portend the imminent destruction whose scope not even he could have imagined?

THE HOUSE to which Mother brought us in Sighet had many hardships. It was a house of poverty where bread was literally a rare commodity, where I slept on a straw sack. (I remember that when the straw had to be changed, usually before Passover, it was a struggle to acquire the money to change it.) Grandfather, who, as I mentioned, was a great scholar, was a Belzer *chasid*. There was only one other such chasid in the town of Sighet; the majority of the Jews were either Sigheter or Viznitser *chasidim*. So Grandfather was the "wrong chasid," and therefore, for many years, even though everyone recognized him as a scholar, he did not have an official position. Only later in his life did some members of the community council—particularly two: Beryl Landau and Shlomo Weiss—arrange for Grandfather to be given some support, albeit very meager, and ostensibly he was placed in charge of supervising the community schools, the *kols chadorim*, which meant that he visited them several times a week, spoke to the teachers, perhaps explained some difficult passages of the Talmud to them, got acquainted with the students, and suggested promotions. When I came to

Sighet, I also became a student of one of Grandfather's schools.

The money that was given to Grandfather for this work was hardly sufficient for even a small family, and it was almost impossible to support a household that had suddenly increased by four new members—Mother, myself, and my two sisters. His was a household that already had two unmarried daughters in their late twenties, which at that time, of course, was considered beyond marriageable age. Above all, in those regions, one had to have a considerable sum for a dowry to marry off a daughter, and Grandfather had not enough for a single daughter, let alone two. Now, with our being there as well, he had to worry about our day-to-day existence; he had neither the patience nor the opportunity to procure dowries, and the daughters remained unmarried.

The older of my two aunts, Channa Yitte, became desperate, I think, and got married but faced tragedy, which added more pain and tension in the house. She married a cousin, Yisroel Yehuda Katina, who was suffering, so it seems, from an inherited disease, which his family knew but Grandfather did not know when he arranged the marriage. There was some hint of trouble to come when Grandfather's brother, the grandfather of the *chosen*, the bridegroom, was not enthusiastic about the *shidduch*, the match. Only later did we understand that while he clearly could not come out against the marriage of his grandchild, he already knew the fatal nature of the disease. Yisroel Yehuda died when he was twenty-seven, leaving two orphans, a boy and a girl. For a while the two children and their mother lived with us, which made Grandfather's house even more crowded, and more edgy. Later, Channa

Yitte moved in with her in-laws in a village close to Khust—and finally she perished in the gas chamber at Auschwitz. Hitler took her because of her children, and they were gassed together. As a rule, mothers went with children.

The other sister, Ethel, stayed and never got married. Not being married, she had every reason to resent our presence in Grandfather's house, and as she occasionally disciplined me I was convinced that she disliked me especially. I remember that at age seven or eight, I found an outlet for my negative feelings toward this aunt. According to custom, during the reading of the Torah in the synagogue—or, more correctly, after completing a portion of the reading—a *mi'sheberach* is made, a prayer for someone's recovery from a sickness or some other supplication. I figured that it should work the other way, too— negatively. If you curse somebody or pray for that person's having a seizure, or some other misfortune, I surmised, that also would be achieved. And in my child's imagination, I thought that my aunt who disciplined me disliked me, and I used the occasion of the Torah reading to say a negative prayer against her. Only much later, when we arrived together on the ramp at Auschwitz, did I learn that this same Aunt Ethel did not in fact despise me but was deeply caring, and respectful of my learning.

In a sense, not being married was lucky for Ethel because she had no children, and when she arrived in Auschwitz with us she apparently survived the selection by Mengele only to die somewhere else in the concentration camps. I lost track of her and have never been able to find out what actually happened to her.

We were three siblings. One of my sisters, also called

Channa Yitte, was three years older than I, and my other
sister, Leitzu, was four years older. Leitzu suffered from
something like cerebral palsy; I don't know exactly what
it was. I remember that my mother told me that when my
sister was little they had taken her to doctors in Vienna,
but there was no hope for recovery. Her hands and feet
were always curled and she could not straighten them out;
she could not stand and could not grasp anything. She
used to lie, all the time, on a bed with a sack cover, and
her needs had to be attended to. She could not feed herself
or perform any other everyday activities; but intellectually,
she was superior. She knew several languages, knew exactly what was going on in the house, and participated in
conversations with great intelligence. She liked it when
someone held her hands—"smoothing," we called it, for
when her hands were held she felt a sense of their being
smooth. She particularly liked for me to come and sit with
her and hold her hands. But her sickness added tension in
the house and I suffered also, psychologically. I remember
that she could go out only in a carriage, but the carriage
had to be much bigger than a normal carriage for infants.
When we went out in the street and I walked with her,
children used to taunt her, saying, "Such a big girl, still
in a carriage!" Leitzu was apparently already accustomed
to this insult, but it pained me every time.

A LACK of income, two girls unmarried, as well as my
sister's sickness and the hatred that Mother instilled in us
against Father, who was still living in another city, should
have made life almost unbearable at home. Yet when I
recall my childhood, I would say that it was not an un-

pleasant one—for I took to learning, and learning took to me.

I was considered a child prodigy, someone with whom the entire community identified and in whom it took pride, and this lifted our spirits at home. In a sense, it justified Mother's coming to Grandfather's. Had I stayed with Father, I probably would not have developed into a precocious child; and as it was, the community generously identified itself with its *ilui*, its child prodigy, the ilui of Sighet. My precociousness compensated greatly, both at home and outside, for the struggle and hardships that we experienced at home.

The community in Sighet expressed its appreciation of my learning in different ways. There were no cars in Sighet. When you called a doctor you had to provide him with transportation, with a horse and buggy. Whenever I walked in the street and met Dr. Krauss (the husband of Dr. Gizelle Perl, who survived the Holocaust and later wrote a book about being a doctor in Auschwitz), he would stop his horse and buggy and pick me up, a gesture that showed he approved of my learning and acknowledged my special status. And when Leizer Hoch, a learned butcher, went to the slaughterhouse every Wednesday, walking out of the town with a book in his hand, if he saw me he stopped. If it was an ordinary weekday, he would give me a single coin, a *leu*. If it was *Rosh Chodesh*, the beginning of a new Jewish month, he would give me two lei. On *Chol Hamoed*, the intermediate days of Passover or *Sukkot*, I might get five. People on the street used to stop me, or come up to the window of our house to look at me. I really felt a part of the community. It was the love of the community that sustained me, or perhaps created defenses for me, allowing me to overcome the circumstances in the house, the unbearable situation it could so easily have become.

The community's support of me was to extend even into the concentration camp at Gross-Rosen, where there were Polish Jewish *kapos* who generally were not kind to Hungarian Jews, which for this purpose included our area, too. These kapos met people who told them of my Talmudic knowledge and they treated me better for it, and now and then gave me an extra piece of bread.

AT THE age of four, then, I came to Sighet and joined the kols chadorim. Apparently, my *ivre*, my Hebrew reading, was not yet proficient, because I remember that the third-grade teacher, Reb Alter, used to listen to my reading to help me practice it and become more fluent in it—usually an indication that there are still flaws. No wonder that this same Reb Alter never accepted the idea that I was different from or had a better mind for learning than other students. Years later, he used to repeat, "When he was my student, he wasn't better; he was worse even!" "Worse" meant worse than my nearest rival, Naftali Elimelech Schiff, who somehow, at the age of eight or nine, developed a mental illness and disappeared as a competitor.

So it seems that at the age of four, beginning to study Chumash, I did not display anything special or extraordinary. That started when I was five. I say this on the strength of certain sayings which, years later, were still repeated in the community as things I had said when I was five. I was then sitting all day long in *cheder*, in school, under the tutelage of the teacher, reading out loud from the Chumash, with the commentary of Rashi, the foremost medieval commentator, whose annotations on the Bible are based on the *Midrash*, some sources of which may date back to the first century. I remember particularly the biblical story concerning Jacob and his daughter Dinah. The text says that when Jacob met his brother Esau, after having fled from him, Jacob had eleven children—his eleven sons. Rashi asks, "Where was Dinah? Jacob had a daughter as well, and this makes twelve." Rashi explains that Dinah is not mentioned because Jacob was afraid to have her meet Esau—the medieval Jew's perennial fear of having a non-Jew meet a Jewish woman—and so packed her in a box. I remember that I asked in school, "If someone asked how many children my mother has, would we say two because I am not there? What difference does it make where I am? So long as I exist I should be counted part of the family; and so, too, with Dinah." Apparently, this incident developed wings in the community.

Another saying that was quoted in my name, at the age of five, concerned the manna in the desert. According to tradition, one could sense any taste one desired in the manna, with the exception of garlic. The reason given for the exception is that garlic is harmful to pregnant women. When our teacher recounted this to us, I challenged him, arguing that if the taste of the manna was determined by the selection of the eater, and if the manna potentially contained all tastes, and whatever one desired one had, why couldn't one choose garlic also? If it is harmful to a pregnant woman, let the woman not desire its taste! The teacher did not know the answer. Neither did his supervisor (who was not Grandfather). "The whole town was stirred," as the Book of Ruth says. A simple question had been asked by a five-year-old and nobody seemed to know the answer. Eventually an answer from tradition was produced. I do not remember who quoted it, but it was said that it is written in a book that the mere potential taste of garlic is sufficient to be harmful to a pregnant woman, even if she was not to evoke the taste itself. I do not know how many people were convinced by the answer, but the question raised my reputation in town.

BUT THAT did not yet make me exceptional. That I date from the time I surprised Grandfather while we were in the bath. We did not have running water in our house; hardly anyone in Sighet had running water. If we needed hot water, we heated it on the stove. But there was a public bath, in addition to the *mikveh* (the ritual bath), with separate rooms containing bathtubs, two to a room. Of course, this sort of bathing cost about five times more than going to the mikveh. Grandfather used to go there once a week to take a bath and took me along. We shared the same bathtub, and the man who was in charge of the bath, Froim the Beder, who knew Grandfather, looked away and allowed me to go in with him for one price.

I remember we were coming out of the bath, toweling ourselves dry, and I told Grandfather that I thought I remembered the names of all our forefathers, the patriarchs, who lived from the time of Adam to the time of David the King. I was already aware of the *mishnah* in the *Sayings of the Fathers* that counts ten generations from Adam to Noah and ten from Noah to Abraham, but the mishnah does not list the names. I don't remember whether I did indeed know all of them, or missed a few and Grandfather filled them in, but anyhow I came very close. I added, "Avraham, Yitzhak, Yaakov, Yehuda, Peretz, Chetzron, Ram, Amindav, Nachshon, Salmon, Boaz, Oved, Yishai, and David" beyond the generations mentioned in the mishnah—thirty-four names in all, which I remember to this day. We were not supposed to study or mention holy names in the bathhouse, but Grandfather was so stunned that I had gathered up these names on my own, consulting the Book of Chronicles (of which we had a torn copy at home), that he could not resist allowing me to list them then and there.

He shared the story with others, and this was the beginning of people coming up to me in the street to ask, "Who was the twentieth person?" or, "Who was the twentieth grandchild of Adam?" As time went on and I acquired knowledge of the Talmud, the questions persisted and changed accordingly: not "Who was whose son," but "How does the forty-eighth page of the Talmud begin?" "How does it end?" "How many times is Rabbi Yosef mentioned in such-and-such a tractate?" "What does he say the forty-fourth time?" and so on. Sometimes, not very often, a person would place a needle on a word in the Talmud and ask, "What is written at this spot on the pages beneath?"

I recall that I once came to Visheva, the hometown of my future wife, Tzipora, and met a Mr. Jakobowitz, who was engaged in the lumber business. He told me that he would give me fifty lei, a considerable sum, if I told him the sixty-fourth statement of Rava, the famous Talmudic sage, in Tractate *Bava Metzia*. I told him, and then stretched out my hand, expecting him to give me the money. He looked at me and said, "How do I know that you gave me the right answer?" It was a logical objection, but of course I could not leave it at that, so I said, "Well, if I tell you the twentieth, the twenty-fifth, the fortieth, and so on, will you give me the money?" In this same vein, at the age of nine, I learned by heart two hundred *dapim* (folios)—four hundred pages of Talmud—with Rashi's commentary and that of his disciples the Tosafists, and for this received a prize, provided by the Feuerstein family of Boston, which was enough to support the whole family for a week or two.

So excited was I when I received the money that I rushed out of the room, forgetting to thank the examining rabbis. When I was summoned back into the room with the reproach "Don't you even say thank you?" I was deeply embarrassed. But I quickly got out of the embarrassment by quoting to them from the Talmud, from the very same tractate on which they had examined me, from *Bava Metzia* 12a. There the Talmud first quotes the rule "An object found by a man's son or daughter, who is a minor . . . belongs to the man himself." "For what reason?" the Talmud inquires. "Because," explains Samuel, "when the minor finds it he brings it hurriedly to his father. [It is therefore assumed that when he picked the object up he did so on behalf of his father.] . . . a minor has no right to acquire anything for himself." "If I have no right to acquire anything for myself," I exclaimed triumphantly to the examining rabbis, "if I am merely a courier, then let my grandfather thank you!" The somber rabbis could not resist a forgiving chuckle.

When I was in Visheva, I of course visited the rabbi of the town, the renowned chasidic rebbe, Rabbi Menachem Mendel Hager. He examined me, and apparently was sufficiently impressed that he told his family that such a son-in-law he would like to have for his granddaughter Tzipora. Years passed, the world went up in flames, the Jews of the region were deported to Auschwitz, and the survivors dispersed across the world. I met Tzipora in New York in 1949. We both attended Brooklyn College, and after graduation in 1953, we were married.

IN 1942 I visited Ungvár (Uzhgorod), the largest city in Transcarpathia. I had a cousin living there who invited me to visit him. The Jews in Ungvár were a little more affluent than the Jews of Sighet. They lived more comfortably and could afford to be more generous. While I was in Ungvár, my learning caught the attention of members of the Stern family, well-to-do merchants, who arranged to buy me a complete set of clothing, from top to bottom, hat to shoes. That was the first time that I had a completely new wardrobe rather than old clothes made over to fit me. Whenever I recall my visit to Ungvár I cannot but feel humbled by the warmth and affection that I experienced there. The people's love for learning was boundless, and I was their beneficiary as the young man who concretized it.

In Ungvár I met a Jew whose activity most faithfully embodied the activity that the Talmud ascribes to God. "Since the day the Temple was destroyed," reports Ulla, a third-century scholar of the land of Israel, "the Holy One, blessed be He, has nothing in this world save the four cubits of *halakhah*, of Law" (Babylonian Talmud, *Berakhot* 8a). The generosity of the Sterns in buying me my new clothes, I was told, came as a result of a request from this man, Rabbi Schlesinger, who was a distant relative of theirs. Rabbi Schlesinger was a great *mefalpel*, a man who liked to pursue scholarly arguments for argument's sake, often positing farfetched possibilities. Rabbi Schlesinger was engaged in no activity other than learning. He had no time to make a living and lived in extreme poverty. When I visited his two cramped rooms (where he lived with his wife, a dutiful, short, and humble woman who seemed to blend in perfectly with her husband's activity), I could not resist thinking of another statement in the Talmud about another rabbi, Hanina ben Dosa (first century, of the land of Israel): "Rabbi Judah said in the name of Rav, 'Every day a divine voice goes forth from Mount Horeb and proclaims, 'The whole world is sustained for the sake of my son Hanina, and Hanina my son subsists on a *kab* [a small measure] of carobs from one week to the next.' "

As soon as I came to Ungvár, Rabbi Schlesinger took me under his wing (he had no children of his own), taking me for long walks and engaging me in incessant Talmudic conversations that might range over any subject, any topic at all. I remember one day we started our walk without a clear agenda, without agreeing beforehand on a topic for our conversation. Rabbi Schlesinger suggested that we turn into a side street, and that the first object we encountered should become our topic. As might have been expected, the first thing we encountered was a horse and buggy. Without a pause, Rabbi Schlesinger inquired: Why are we Jews allowed to maintain horses when, according to Jewish law, one is not allowed to trade in animals that one is forbidden to eat? (Trading may lead to eating—and horses are among the forbidden animals.) That horsemeat was not generally eaten, at least not in our society, was not a satisfactory answer for Rabbi Schlesinger. He was looking for a more profound dialectical answer, the details of which I do not remember. I do remember, however, that he made reference to the biblical exhortation that a king should not multiply horses—implying that if the horses are not too many the king and presumably also the commoners are allowed to breed and maintain them.

GRANDFATHER FOUND himself completed in me. I can say that he fulfilled himself through my knowledge and learning. None of his own children—he had five sons—were real scholars and, in a way, I compensated for them. Grandfather took particular pleasure in the public event of a distinguished rabbi's coming to town. He would take me to the rabbi, in the most public of places, and have questions asked of me. I know that he enjoyed our being together because he resisted my leaving. There was talk in the family that I should go elsewhere to study in a *yeshiva*, which would have relieved some of the economic burden on Grandfather. He refused, even though things were very difficult for him.

My sick sister, Leitzu, died in 1941. Since she could not stand on her feet, she eventually got water in her lungs, which choked her. I still remember holding her hands the day she died. With her death the household was reduced by one, and if I had gone away it would have been even easier for Grandfather financially. During the war, the community could not pay him even the meager sum he had been promised. Nevertheless, he always found excuses, reasons, why I should stay with him.

Grandfather also defended me against detractors. I remember particularly one evening when I was sleeping in the living room (which also served as a bedroom) and an uncle was visiting us. I could see Grandfather's agitation; I recognized it when Grandfather began to walk around and had his thumb stuck in his vest, under his armpit. I had woken up, and I remember the gist of the conversation.

Not having been born in Sighet had protected me from having to go to school. There was already compulsory education at that time; everybody had to attend the first four elementary grades. That meant going to secular schools, which people like me tried to avoid. In my case this was relatively easy. Since I had not been born in the country and had no birth certificate, I was not counted as a resident; and every year, before the school year started, when the principal or some other representative of the school knocked at the door to ask if there were any school-age children in the house, my mother could conveniently say no—especially since I was actually in the *beis medrash*, the study hall.

But in 1940, both Sighet and my birthplace had come under the Hungarian occupation. In the beginning, Mother still tried to deny that I was there, but soon it became dangerous because the authorities might have found records of my birth. Mother confessed that she had a school-age boy, and soon afterward I received a notice to attend school. Since I was by then much older than seven, the age when children began school, Grandfather went to ask the president of the community, Mr. Josewitz, to intervene with the authorities so that I might take private classes and an examination—reading, writing, and a little arithmetic.

Then the problem of a teacher arose. We didn't have money to pay anyone, so we had to find a volunteer. The logical candidate was a fellow who used to come to Grandfather's Talmud lessons, his *shiurim*, which he gave at the Kahanishe synagogue five times a week in the evening after prayers. About a dozen people came to listen, including Shimi Weiss, who was a student in the gymnasium. I recall being told that Shimi Weiss declined to teach me on the grounds that in Sighet a great number of the Jewish youth became secular, Communist or Socialist, and he was afraid that if he taught me and I strayed from the proper path, people would blame him for my irreligiosity. He tactfully declined. It turned out, interestingly enough, that this same Shimi Weiss who used to come to Grandfather's class—either because he wanted to hide his Communist activity or because he still enjoyed a good study session—became the mayor of Sighet when the Communists occupied the town after the war.

In the end, we recruited a girl from the neighborhood by the name of Rutzi Kratz, who did not survive. She helped me, and somehow I managed to pass the test. I obviously didn't learn much; I was not really able to read Hungarian properly, but I knew enough to look at a newspaper and read the headlines. At night sometimes I would come home from a full day's study and sit down at the table, my elbows on the table, my head resting on my fists, and get as deeply absorbed in the newspaper as I did in a religious text. I could make out the gist of the article.

One night when the uncle I have mentioned saw me doing this, he complained to Grandfather, saying that my religious behavior was wanting because I read newspapers. He went on to pile up a whole list of religious infractions which, even among the very Orthodox, would sound absurd today. I had become modern; I ate with a fork, unlike most people, who ate with their hands; I curled my earlocks; I was always trying to make sure I had a crease in my pants—things of this sort. This was the night I awoke to Grandfather's pacing, his thumb stuck in his vest.

Grandfather defended me, saying that he knew what I was doing and that he could not be expected to deprive me of coming home at night and looking at a newspaper, particularly in these troubled times. Neither my accuser nor my defender knew how limited my understanding of the newspaper was. As to the other alleged infractions, Grandfather dismissed them. He didn't see these actions as elements that amounted to a trend. It was an attempt to defend me at all costs, because he really needed me.

AS A chasid, Grandfather had an external appearance indistinguishable from that of other chasidim. He wore a *kapote*, a big caftan, and a big fringed garment, an *arba kanfos*, which wasn't always clean, and he smoked a long pipe, which sometimes he could not light himself and would ask one of his grandchildren to light up for him. His mustache was darkened from smoking. His whole demeanor was that of a local chasid. On Saturday, the Sabbath, he wore a special *shtreimel*, a fur hat, which during the Nazi period he almost risked his life to wear in the street. During the days between the arrival of the Nazis and when we were taken to the ghetto, he insisted on wearing his shtreimel outdoors, even though he knew it meant danger.

Grandfather dared to do this even though he was generally a *dershrockener*, a man afraid of his own shadow and especially of people in uniform, including the postman, and people in authority. Before Christmas, Grandfather used to entertain the postman, treating him to a shot of schnapps. Looking at his face at those times, one could see the great effort that he mustered to control his fear. A man of great native intelligence, and with a vast knowledge of Jewish law, Grandfather was frequently chosen to sit on an arbitration panel. Sometimes when the arbitration failed and the litigants went back to the courts, Grandfather was asked to appear as a witness. When that happened, nights before his appearance in court he could not sleep, afraid of what the judge might do to him. People in uniform and in authority were, generally, anti-Semitic, as was the general population. Most Jews had no choice but to become accustomed to their attitude and behavior. The contact of day-to-day business lessened their fear. Grandfather, who had no regular dealings with non-Jews, felt only terror in their presence.

I remember that when walking with Grandfather in the streets of Sighet, particularly after dark, we were alert to the boisterous noise of young people reveling, for fear that they might beat us up or at least pull our beards and *peyos* (earlocks). Grandfather felt a little more secure when there was a woman among the young people. In the presence of a female companion, he reasoned, the men would be more restrained. (In his mind, women were less given to cruelty than men, a proposition that proved false. Women concentration camp guards were no less brutal than their male counterparts.) As usual, Grandfather found support for what he believed in the Talmud. The tractate *Bava*

Kama, page 60a, relates: "Our rabbis taught: when dogs howl it is a sign that the Angel of Death has come to town; when the dogs frolic it is a sign that Elijah the prophet has come to town." "This is true," the Talmud explains, "only if there is no female among them." Dogs were popular among the rabbis of the Talmud, and most rabbis had positive opinions about them. In Eastern Europe, however, dogs became associated with Gentile oppression and were feared by Jews, probably because of the practice of some Gentile authorities of inciting their dogs to attack Jews.

Grandfather was also a *farfroirener,* a man who suffered terribly from the cold—not surprising in the harsh winter cold of the Carpathian Mountains. He was always amazed that the rabbinic sages, who instituted blessings for all sorts of pleasurable sensations, had not prescribed a prayer to be said upon coming in from the cold. Of course, the sages of the Mishnah and the Talmud lived far from the cold of the Carpathian Mountains.

So attached was Grandfather to other chasidim, even if they were not of his kind, that he rejected rabbinic offers which would have relieved him of his chronic poverty, since these offers came from communities that had few if any chasidim. The Jews in these communities were *Oberlander,* fierce in their religious observance but not adherents of the chasidic customs. Grandfather preferred poverty to living among non-chasidim.

NOT ONLY in dress but in almost all respects—his manner of speech, worldview, and the like—Grandfather was indistinguishable from any other chasid. But when he

learned, when he taught, there was in him a spark of ge-
nius and uniqueness. I do not know where his special
method came from. While everyone around him studied
the Talmud in a casuistic way, going against the grain of
the text, reading meanings into the text in a convoluted
way, Grandfather tried to be as faithful as possible to the
actual words of the text itself. One might call it a scientific, objective way of studying. Since he had not studied
in a yeshiva but was self-taught, Grandfather was not affected by the casuistic method of study developed in ye-
shivas during the last few centuries, and he followed what
the text actually said. His youngest brother, also a great
scholar, Rabbi Leib Weiss from Tyachevo (whose picture
on the ramp in Auschwitz has been reproduced, uniden-
tified, in many books on the Holocaust, including the
Encyclopedia Judaica [volume 8, page 880]), was very
erudite but did not follow the *peshat*, the simple, unem-
bellished meaning of the text, as Grandfather did. I recall
exchanges between him and Grandfather in which Grandfather expressed annoyance that his brother was deviating,
forcing the text, not letting the words speak for themselves.

I remember that after Grandmother died of cancer,
when I was seven or eight years old (another source of
tension and hardship in the house), Mother wanted me to
learn *mishnayot* (chapters of the Mishnah, the most authoritative early Rabbinic text), which is customary after
a death in the family, and I learned a chapter every day.
When I got to the tractate *Kilayim*, which includes laws
about mixing different species, I didn't understand it. I
burst into tears. Mother asked Grandfather, "Why don't
you explain it to him? Why do you let him cry?" And

Grandfather said, "He knows what I know. What can I tell him?" He meant that he could repeat to me the meaning of the text as perceived by the commentators; but I wouldn't accept the commentators' interpretation because I felt it was too convoluted, too forced. And beyond that, Grandfather could not go. He helped me understand the commentators, but he could not assuage my pain, my non-acceptance of this kind of interpretation.

Of course, Grandfather was limited in his scholarly means. He did not have enough books, and certainly not enough manuscripts and first editions—things we now have in abundance—to perfect a critical method. Grandfather also had some religious restrictions: there is a certain casuistry built into Talmudic reasoning and, as I learned years later, the text itself is often not straightforward. Therefore, even if you're faithful to its literal meaning, you have to give it a convoluted interpretation, unless you part company with the text or interpret an earlier text in a manner that diverges from its reception in later tradition, something that Grandfather would never have done. Years later, when I did sometimes reject a convoluted text and allow myself to interpret it differently, I remember what Grandfather said in warning: "When you study a text, you have to have faith that the author cannot make a mistake. Otherwise, why bother understanding the text? You could simply dismiss it by saying that the author made a mistake." I follow his method, but I follow it without the restrictions he imposed upon it, and I use modern means of libraries and photocopies and photographs of manuscripts and first printed editions, and so on. This has radically changed my learning, but I am still following in Grandfather's footsteps. I often wonder now what Grandfather's reaction would be. I say this while sitting in my office, where his picture gazes at me. What would he say to my books, to my interpretations of the Talmud? I hope and pray that with his good sense of peshat—of intuiting what the text itself says—although he would not do it himself, he would nevertheless be sympathetic to what I have to say.

Grandfather published nothing and left nothing in manuscript. The conflict between what his colleagues valued and what he stood for made him believe that what he had to say would not be appreciated. Alas! He might have changed their approach. But his scholarly barrenness also may have been a result of an inner inclination, strengthened by his environment, not to challenge, not to go against the grain. It is a characteristic I may have inherited from him, except that the society in which I live encourages writing and stimulates the desire to challenge.

DESPITE THE high esteem in which the *Kabbalah* (Jewish mystical literature) was held among the chasidim in Sighet, I never saw Grandfather studying Kabbalah. (I was too young for these studies myself; in some quarters, forty is considered the minimum age for commencing esoteric studies.) Nor do I remember having seen in our house books like the *Zohar* (*The Book of Splendor*), the classical book of the Kabbalah. We did have some secondary works of Kabbalah, books of the chasidic masters, particularly those to whom Grandfather felt close, but I do not have any recollection of Grandfather's having studied them with the same intensity and zeal with which he studied the Talmud, the *Shulchan Aruch* (the authoritative

Jewish law code), or even the books of Rabbi Moses Sofer (1763–1839) who was not exactly a *mitnaged* (an anti-chasid), but not a chasid either. Among the books we did have in the house was the *Noam Elimelech*, a book by Rabbi Elimelech of Lyzensk (a Polish chasidic master, 1717–1787) that was highly regarded in our region for both its intellectual and its mystical power. The book appeared in two editions: one with stars printed in the intervals between sentences, and one without stars. The stars were supposed to indicate deep, secret, esoteric meaning that even the learned could decipher only after first going to the mikveh. I remember that one Friday afternoon, after visiting the mikveh—a required preparation for welcoming the Sabbath among chasidim—I took out the *Noam Elimelech*, with its stars, intending to try my hand at deciphering them. As soon as Grandfather became aware of what I was doing, I realized that I had brought him into a predicament. He clearly would have preferred that I study Talmud, or its related literature, but did not know how to explain this to me without diminishing the aura of holiness associated with the esoteric book. He was delighted when I was distracted by a call to perform a household errand needed to complete the preparations for the Sabbath (rather unusual at that late hour), and I took it as a sign that I was not yet ready for such a lofty undertaking. I closed the book and have not really opened it since.

FROM GRANDFATHER, I believe, I inherited my sense of humor, which stood us both in good stead in times of trouble. During the evening Talmud lessons that he taught, Grandfather used to exchange jokes with his students as an occasional relief from close to two hours' concentration on difficult Talmudic subjects and their interpretation. I listened, spellbound and with great pleasure, although eventually the jokes became repetitive and a little stale. Grandfather was really a raconteur, possessing a rich repertoire of jokes and knowing how to use them. He did not contribute new jokes, nor was he apt to create humorous situations or comical remarks, but he had a good memory; whatever jokes he heard or read he remembered, and he had the ability to recall them at the appropriate moment. The same can be said of me; I must have acquired the ability from him.

What surprised me most was how free these jokes were from constraints, religious or otherwise. The rule was: Anything goes. What generally would have been considered heretical or immodest was, in the joke, utterly forgiven or even encouraged. One of the "hit" jokes was the story of a Jew who was trying to convince his friend of the importance of monotheism, of One God who rules all. "What do I care?" said the other Jew. "Do I have to support them? Let there be many." Unintentionally, the joke cheapens the belief in monotheism, the cornerstone of Judaism, but it was nevertheless tolerated and enjoyed. I once titled a lecture on this kind of joke "Irreverent Jokes in a Reverent Society."

From Grandfather I may also have inherited the tendency, after a speech or a lecture, to ask a listener how well I performed. While I am not as crass as Grandfather was (for which he was criticized by the very few who were not sympathetic to him), I do the same, though more circumspectly, for example, asking the listener whether he or she could hear me, whether the loudspeaker was functioning properly, when in fact my intention was to solicit an opinion about the quality of my performance.

GRANDFATHER WAS generally very affectionate, though not in a demonstrative way. All those years I was with him, I never heard him complain about having to support us all. When his income became so meager that he had to go around borrowing money, he told people of his plight, but never in my presence did he complain that we were a burden. I think that, basically, I was not a burden to him. He felt the bond between us through the similarity of our learning. To this day I feel that if he did not implant in me the sense of peshat, which is my life's work, he certainly strengthened it. The learning cemented us together. The sense of wholeness he felt in my presence of course made my life at home quite pleasant despite the many hardships, economic and political, that my family and the Jewish community then faced—hardships that ultimately led to their destruction.

GRANDFATHER RELIVED his life through me, which made his life easier. Of course, there was no consideration given at that time to what effect that had on me. Looking back, I think that knowing that my achievements made my family, and the community, happy or unhappy put a burden on me, a need to succeed and to be loved. Even to this day a certain desire for recognition may be stronger in me than in others because it was always connected with my very existence; it served as a safeguard to ward off the many difficulties in which I found myself.

Another influence upon my learning was my childhood desire to study not only Talmud but other subjects, including secular subjects, to the extent that every morning when I prayed the words "O Lord, give our hearts wisdom so that we may understand and be intelligent," I used to look up at the window, which was the symbol of the outside world, meaning that I wanted God to give me understanding and wisdom to know also what goes on in the world at large—at least in the scholarly and cultural world.

I remember that after the war my strong desire was to go to school and study secular subjects; but when I had the opportunity to attend college and graduate school, and I excelled in philosophy, somehow I went back to the Talmud, which gave me a sense of security. I wasn't really secure with any subject except the Talmud.

MOTHER DID not reconcile herself so easily to her plight. I know she took pride in my achievement, but her inner life was still torn. Occasionally, when she was in a particularly bad mood, a certain skepticism and pessimism overcame her, and she directed it against all of us, including me. If I refused to do something or she was angry with me, she would say that when she would be covered with green velvet, by which she meant the grass of her grave, I would not even say *Kaddish*, the mourner's prayer, for her. It was a kind of hyperbole; she didn't mean it and nobody took it seriously, but it expressed frustration. In

Sighet, it was unthinkable to neglect saying Kaddish even if you wanted to, and certainly I was far from not wanting to say Kaddish for her.

Ironically, in retrospect, Mother was right. I did not say Kaddish for her: she died in Auschwitz. In fact, I discovered only after the war that she was dead, after the eleven-month period for reciting the Kaddish prayer had passed. I do know the date when we came to Auschwitz and, of course, I keep the *yahrzeit*, the anniversary of her death, and I say Kaddish for her then. I do the same for Grandfather, because I know now when they were killed. I do not say Kaddish for my sister Channa Yitte or my father because I do not know when they died. But I do remember them during the *Yizkor* service, which we say four times a year on holidays. I remember my close family members who passed away. Since there is also a special passage for martyrs, I mention them twice, as family members and as martyrs. I always find it a bit irritating to say the prayer's promise that I will give charity so that they will rest in the place of the righteous—as if they don't already deserve that place.

Mother, whose name was Feige, was a proud lady. She walked erect and tall, but was deeply wounded by the arrows of destiny. I remember that every year before the High Holy Days there was a crisis in the house. Mother used to go to the synagogue every Saturday morning wearing a hat that was a slight deviation from the religious norms of her social class, which required a *tichel*, a kerchief. She sat in the first row of the women's section and made a point of praying loudly, so that the women who sat behind her, even if they did not have a prayer book or did not know how to pray, followed the service.

During the year there was no problem. Few women came to the synagogue and Mother could sit in the first row undisturbed. But during the High Holy Days the community took advantage of the many requests for seats by selling them. We, of course, had no money to buy seats. Some families owned seats, called *steit*, and passed them from generation to generation. Especially desirable were the seats of the first row of the women's section, for they afforded a view of the men's activities below. Mother insisted on occupying the same seat all year round, pressuring Grandfather to use his connections with the members of the community council to prevent them from selling her seat for the High Holy Days. As far as I remember, he never failed. Several members of the council were sympathetic to Grandfather's dilemma and prevailed upon their colleagues to leave her seat in the first row unsold; but not until the last minute, until the eve of the holiday, did we know for sure. In the meantime, Mother would be tense, and this was passed on to the whole family.

GRANDFATHER SERVED me as a father, and I had no contact with my father for years. That was what Mother, and maybe Grandfather, too, wanted. But I subsequently heard that in 1940 he was deported to the Polish side of the border. There was an outburst of deportation of about eighteen thousand Jews who lived near the Polish border in the Carpathian Mountains. They were taken illegally on the pretext that they were not citizens, even though they were born locally, and were deported to Kamenets-Podolski, a town in Russian-occupied Poland where Jews were shot and killed. However, Father succeeded in es-

caping and came back to live in a community not far from
Sighet. I visited him there afterward when life became very
difficult for me in Sighet, where teenagers were required
to do pre-military service every Friday. Mother and
Grandfather wanted to spare me this, so they sent me to
Father, and I got to know him, but only for a short time.
I came back to Sighet, and he stayed where he was. In
1944 he was deported again, to Auschwitz, and on the
train he succeeded in writing me an encouraging postcard,
which reached me in the ghetto where we had been taken.
I was told by some people that from Auschwitz he was
taken to Warsaw to clean up the rubble and from there,
on his way to Dachau, he stepped off the wrong side of a
train, was attacked by SS dogs, and died from that.

BECAUSE SIGHET was situated near a river, it was
among the towns permitted by Jewish law to perform divorces. Proximity to a body of water was considered for
a long time the most reliable means of geographical identification, and Jewish law requires that the locale of a divorce be identified this way. This drew to Sighet couples
who were about to be divorced, and brought in some rev-
enue to the community, or at least to the rabbis who performed the divorces. For some reason that I cannot fully
explain, I was never asked to be present at divorce proceedings, even though, of course, I had studied the laws
of divorce. Perhaps because of the mutual recriminations
that the couple to be divorced hurled at each other, which
often touched on marital relations, I, a bachelor, could not
be present, even though I was about to be ordained. Similarly, in the shiurim (Talmud lessons) in which I partici-

pated, or which I even led, whenever we came to a passage that contained erotic material I left the table. The mishnah of *Hagigah* (2:1) prohibits expounding the laws of forbidden sexual relations (Leviticus 18:6 ff.) before three or more persons, married or unmarried. The fear is that dwelling on the sexual content may lead to misconduct. Sending me out, however, was not motivated by this mishnah, since the others that remained and continued were more than three. Rather it was a sign of that society's labeling the unmarried immature and not ready for the study of such subjects.

Though I was not present at the divorce itself, I was privy to the preliminaries, when the couple were instructed and prepared for the proceedings. Of course, they did not talk to each other directly. Each side spoke through its representative, usually a relative, and the representatives spoke to each other. But the couple could not avoid exchanging glances, and I could not avoid gauging the bitter hatred and disgust they felt for each other. That pained me. The pain was perhaps also due to my imagination, in which I saw not the couple before me but my father and mother, who had gone through a similar experience. Their divorce was probably the only time my parents saw each other after my mother brought us to Sighet.

FROM ALL my troubles in Sighet I found relief in learning. That avenue was not open to my healthy sister, Channa Yitte. Girls in Sighet did not get much schooling. Like me, she craved study. But given the circumstances of that place and time, and my sister being a sort of orphan, since Father was not living with us, after she finished the four elementary classes of secular school she was apprenticed for a few years to slave away at producing girdles, with a view to raising a dowry.

Was she crushed by the adverse conditions around her? Was she morose, difficult to get along with? Did she bemoan her fate? That is not my recollection of her. I remember a girl as happy and outgoing as her friends, who often visited her and who came from more settled homes. Apparently, she, too, derived vicarious compensation from my learning. I learned this later from an American chaplain named Wohlgelernter who had been in Sweden soon after the war ended. He had visited a hospital where there were Jewish girls from Bergen-Belsen dying from typhus. He told me that he had met a girl from Sighet who, although in a daze, spoke of her brother who excelled in the study of Talmud. After he got to know me, he identified her as my sister, Channa Yitte. From him I also learned how much my devotion and ability to study meant to the family and helped to make up for the hardships, difficulties, and deprivation they endured.

I BEGAN this reminiscence by saying that I do not remember when I came to Sighet to live with Grandfather. But I do remember when we parted for the last time—when we were standing in Auschwitz before Josef Mengele, when Mengele signed him away to the right, and me to the left. We arrived there after midnight, Thursday, May 18, 1944 (we did not disembark until morning), on a cattle train where there was hardly room to stand, and I remember Grandfather and Mother would squeeze together to give me room to bend my head over and catch a little sleep. Of course, Grandfather and Mother were awake all throughout the trip. It is the only time I remember that Grandfather asked us, the four of us—my mother, my Aunt Ethel, my sister, who was twenty, and myself—to work for him. That made me realize that he did not know where we were really going. He thought we were going to work. Since he was over eighty years old and unable to work, and the Germans would mistreat him, he asked us to volunteer in his place.

We waited on the train for a few hours, and when the train's locks and doors were opened up, and the sound of "*Hinaus!*" in German rang out—and people speaking different languages, and wearing different striped uniforms, came to meet us—I was the first one to jump off the train, but still heard my Aunt Ethel shout after me, "May the Torah that you have so diligently labored on protect you!" And that was the same aunt who I had thought all along was against me—my imagined enemy!

After jumping off the train, I walked along the Auschwitz platform, the "ramp," with people all around me. Somehow, I must have walked back and forth, because I spotted Mother, who told me that Grandfather was going in another direction and said, "Don't let the old father go alone." She told me to go find him, so I did, and on the way back—and this must all have happened in about three minutes—I met the Chief Rabbi of Sighet, who was also a chasidic rebbe, Yekutiel Yehuda Teitelbaum, a relatively young man in his early thirties, tall, good-looking; and especially since the Germans decreed that Jewish men should cut off their beards, he looked even younger than his age. In Yiddish he said to me, "Let's stick together." And before we had time to exchange another word, we were standing before Mengele.

Mengele grabbed Grandfather, who was eighty years and three months old, by the scruff of his neck and pushed him to the right, and then there was some exchange between Mengele and the Chief Rabbi. I didn't know what they were talking about; I could only surmise that the rabbi wanted to go to the right as well. Since he saw all the prominent members of his congregation, including the president, Mr. Josewitz, going to the right, he may have wanted to go there, too. So Mengele accommodated him and pushed him to the right, and then turned to me, saying, "And you!" Before I could give him an answer, I instinctively ran to the left. Mengele gave me a blow with his whip, and this is how I went to the left and Grandfather went to the right.

WITHIN TWO hours after Mengele parted us, Rabbi Shaye Sigheter was no more. He was consumed by the flames of Auschwitz, by the crematoria. I had always thought that I would be with him until he drew his last breath. I failed him. I was not there. Others, plenty of others, were there. But whether that made his death easier or more difficult I do not know. I was not there to tell.

2

ON THE WAY
Life in the Ghetto

W HEN I think of the Warsaw or Lodz ghettos, I am
embarrassed to claim that I, too, was in a ghetto.
I did not see random killing in the streets or emaciated
siblings sharing their meager rations or babies being torn
away from their mothers. The ghetto in Sighet that I was
in, which lasted for less than a month, was an assemblage
for deportation: an anteroom, a gateway to death. Because
it lasted such a short time, it was never as horrible as other
ghettos. I have no doubt that had we been in the ghetto
longer, our fate would have been very much the same as
that of the Jews in other ghettos.

When I recall my life in the ghetto, I am embarrassed
to admit that my recollection is not as horrendous as
might be assumed. We were seven people in one room.
Everybody had to go to the ghetto; we left everything in
our previous dwelling and went to live with a cousin in a
room with a semblance of a kitchen. Of course, the room
was small. I had to sleep on the floor, but sleeping on the

floor, as a child, after having slept on a straw sack at home, did not impose a special hardship. Of course, in the ghetto we did not have choice food; we had only what we had brought along with us when we left, and even this food was not plentiful. But I didn't eat choice food even before that, so the change was not a radical one. More important, we had to leave our books behind. The lack of books would have meant a total interruption of my previous lifestyle, which consisted of daily, all-day study of the Talmud, enjoying it and living out my life through it. But we found some books locally—the people we came to had some books—and I had enough oral knowledge of the Talmud to sustain me, not only when people came to speak to me but also as I whiled away my time on my own; my routine thus was not terribly interrupted.

The synagogues were all closed. The big synagogue was outside the ghetto, but there were little synagogues, little *shtieblach*. Every home became a *shtiebel*, so I was back in my familiar environment.

True, the ghetto was congested—the ghetto may have consisted of as many as ten thousand Jews occupying four large streets and several small side streets. The main street was the Shlangengass—Snake Street—and we lived at the very edge of the street. The congestion was not unbearable for me. On the contrary, it gave me greater contact with other Jews. In the ghetto I was surrounded by people I had rarely seen before, families I had only heard of. The crowding gave me a chance to meet people from the other two ends of Sighet—the sections of Oberyarish at the eastern edge and Molomkert at the western end. During my stay in Sighet I had visited Oberyarish only once, when my teacher, the Silister Rebbe, moved from the village of Silist, and held a *chanukat habayit* (a housewarming party). He was a man of short build and dark complexion and had very thick glasses, and he opened every study session by reading from a book called *Reishit Chochmah*, by Rabbi Elijah de Vidas, a sixteenth-century scholar of the land of Israel. While sobbing bitterly and uncontrollably, the Silister Rebbe would read to us de Vidas's graphic description of *geihinom*, of hell—ostensibly, though I don't remember his ever saying so, to teach us a lesson of what might happen to us if we were to misbehave or not study diligently. Did the Silister Rebbe have a premonition that soon all hell would break loose, that de Vidas's description of hell was a picnic compared to what actually took place? Was he crying for what was, or for what was going to come? The rebbe, like the other ten thousand Jews of Sighet, with few exceptions, did not return from Auschwitz.

I ALSO rarely visited the Molomkert, the beautiful garden at the edge of the city, adjacent to the river Iza, where young men and young women had romantic rendezvous. For me the river evoked going to *tashlich*, the ritual performed on the second day of Rosh HaShanah, the Jewish New Year (although in my community people also went during the ten days between Rosh HaShanah and Yom Kippur). There by the river we would turn out our pockets and throw the crumbs that might be there into the water, symbolically casting away our sins, as a way of realizing the prophet's saying that God "will hurl all our sins into the depths of the sea" (Micah 7:19). But despite that gesture of seeking forgiveness from sin, God released His wrath and made that innocent, charming ritual discontinue by destroying the people who performed it.

THE DISRUPTION of my education and the lack of classes were not much of a stumbling block. By that time I was on my own. I had stopped going to cheder when I was nine; instead I studied in the *kloiz* (an institution in which no formal instruction took place but where students studied on their own) and practically planned my own education. I studied Talmud and medieval commentaries, and people on the whole knew what I was doing because when they came to the synagogue they engaged in conversation with me. Those who knew actually delved into the subject, and those who didn't know just watched me leafing through the pages.

THE LOSS of childhood and the playfulness that goes with it was not much of a pain to me. By the time I came to the ghetto, at the age of fifteen or sixteen, I was for all intents and purposes already an adult, and was treated as such by the community. I remember that as a child I had been a passionate player of walnuts. The game consisted of throwing the nuts toward a wall; the one who got closest to the wall had the first chance to roll a tar ball at the nuts, which were lined up in the form of head, neck, and the rest of a body. If the ball hit the head, all the nuts belonged to the hitter. But if the ball hit the neck, only the nuts from the neck down went to the hitter, and so on. Once, when I could not have been older than eight or nine, I scored the closest to the wall and, holding the ball in my hand and closing one eye, was aiming at the head. Suddenly, from nowhere, an itinerant preacher with a patriarchal appearance, whom I had never seen before and never saw afterward, passed by, fastened his glance on me, and pointedly exclaimed in Yiddish, "A boy that knows the *sugya of Rabbi Chanina segan haKohanim* [the discussion of Rabbi Chanina, the assistant of the priests—one of the most difficult passages of the Talmud] is not ashamed to play games!" I threw down the ball and never picked it up again. Not having childish fun in the ghetto was thus not one of my hardships.

IN OUR room there was a constant debate between the pessimists and the optimists about what was going to happen to us. The pessimists pointed to the Polish experience: there were many Jews who had escaped from Poland—both Polish Jews and also Hungarian Jews from our region who, like my father, had been expelled over the Carpathian Mountains into Poland and come back. Father never spoke about his experience, but others did. The Jews in Poland were systematically destroyed, shot, killed, deported, burned, and so on. So the pessimists said, "I don't see why our fate should be different from that of the Polish Jews." In general, the Jews of the Carpathians were close culturally, spiritually, and religiously to the chasidic leaders in Galicia, Poland, and in general, most Carpathian Jews of previous generations came from Poland, so they felt there was no reason the Germans would treat us differently. It was just a matter of time.

On the other hand, the optimists pointed out that Hungary was an ally; that Hungary, unlike Poland, had not fought against Germany, and Horthy, the dictator of Hungary, would see to it that his country was not destroyed. Even though he was anti-Semitic, he probably would not want to kill the Jews; instead, he would put them to work. Some said we would work in Hungary, others said we would work in Germany; Germany needed workers. The opinion of my neighbors in the building was primarily the optimistic one, so I did not feel the fear that the ghetto should have imposed on each inhabitant about what ultimately proved to be.

I ALSO confess my zeal for acquiring secular knowledge in addition to the Jewish learning in which I was so immersed. I have already mentioned that during morning prayers, when I prayed for wisdom, I would look up at the window. The window was the symbol of the outside, so when I was inside, especially on winter days when it was dark and there was snow all around, when I felt hemmed in, I looked to the outside, which represented secular knowledge. That's how strong my desire was for secular knowledge.

In my mind, secular knowledge was associated with the German culture and the German language. A lot of Jews from the previous generation who had left their hometowns and gone to Germany came back educated as rabbis or as doctors. Germany was the symbol of education and the place where one acquired it. When our possible destinations were discussed, I even thought that going to Germany might give me the opportunity to go to school there. Of course, I would need to go to the university to get a real education, but even lesser schooling might give me a taste of what goes on in knowledge and scholarship as a whole.

I EVEN received mail in the ghetto. That, too, lent to life a certain modicum of normalcy. There was a special place where mail was distributed, and on one occasion a note was addressed to me. My father had sent me a postcard —apparently written while he was in the cattle car on the way to Auschwitz. He pushed it through a crack in the car and a peasant found and mailed it. The contents of the postcard encouraged me while Father was on the way to Auschwitz.

I did not feel what I should have felt: the enormity, the danger, the death sentence. That might have been, in good part, because I was so absorbed in learning all those years before that it had become second nature. And I continued, even when I was restricted by not having books and not having synagogues. I didn't go out much in the street. I heard that there was a Jewish police, a Jewish council, that some Germans had come to town. Adolf Eichmann, after he had been captured by the Israelis in 1960 and was asked in prison to write his autobiography, mentioned that he was in Sighet, and when he was interrogated about why he went there, he said he had gone to the Carpathian Mountains in

Transylvania for the beautiful women and the good air.

I could not fail to know about the situation outside. People constantly talked about it and mentioned it to me. But it did not register; I chose that it not register. I was too much in another world, or I wanted to be—in the world of learning, which even in the ghetto was still honored and appreciated. So I chose that path.

Not having a father in the ghetto who was active in communal affairs, I was not privy to any affairs of the community. There were people there who had to deal with the Hungarian gendarmerie, and perhaps even with the Germans. But I did not have direct access to these people and, living with a grandfather who was an octogenarian, a Talmud scholar, and a chasid, chose to stay out of the way, not even visiting the streets where I probably would have seen some commotion. I preferred to live in a ghetto within a ghetto, so to speak, and to continue doing what Jews always did—in my case, to continue, through sheer inertia, studying the Talmud and related commentaries. The fact that there were no books was really no hindrance. I had learned enough by heart to continue to study it in my mind. After all, we were the ones who developed the Oral Torah. So while the Hungarian and German authorities left our homes to us, did not invade the inside of our dwellings, although they occasionally overran the streets, I preferred to stay at home and keep to myself.

Even though I knew that the murderers were out there in the streets, so long as I did not confront them face-to-face, so long as I could close my eyes to them, I shut them out, drew an imaginary wall, and denied their existence, and continued to do what I had done all those years, linking myself to the past and continuing to study the same material I had studied since the age of four.

THAT CHANGED on the fateful day of May 14, 1944, when we were driven out of the house, never to reclaim it. We were told on that Sunday morning that we had to leave our house and line up in the street in a row of five—we were five family members: Grandfather, Mother, my sister, my aunt, and myself—and wait in the street for transport. At that time, of course, I lost my home and my imaginary life stopped. I stopped learning. When the surveillance, first by the Hungarians and then by the Germans, was increased, and of course when I was taken the next day to the train and into the sealed car, where the Germans were actually traveling with us, I had no desire or ability to study Torah amid people ready to kill us.

I did not learn on the train, and did not resume formal learning until months after liberation, long after the Germans had disappeared physically, although they were still in my sleep, in my thoughts, and in my fears. Of the train I have very little detailed memory, aside from looking out through the cracks and seeing a peasant harvesting. I thought to myself: Some people harvest produce and some people harvest hatred and murder. The other thing I remember is the ashen faces of the elders, who, after Kassa, on the border between Poland and Hungary, recognized that we were heading to Poland. I had not traveled a lot, the places I visited were not far from Sighet, I had not studied geography and didn't know much about borders, but these people immediately realized that we were going to Poland, and almost in one blow, the optimistic view that we would be taken to Germany was shattered.

THE ONLY visible terror in the ghetto had been the result of the directive proclaimed through emissaries, the Jewish police, that all men must cut off their beards and peyos, ostensibly in the name of hygiene. It is difficult to convey how much terror this struck into the hearts of the people, especially the elderly. The beard and peyos served as a mantle, a shield, a protection against the world—not only spiritually but physically. In shaving them off, the men felt naked to their enemies and left without any protection.

I did not feel so bad about it. On the contrary, the loss of these outward signs of chasidism was a kind of release for me. My lack of anguish did not escape the notice of Rabbi Zalman Leib Gross, one of my teachers, a tall fellow with a jarring voice and a soft heart. I met him in the public bath on the Friday before deportation. Sunday began the deportation, but Friday the public bath was still operating; there was still hot water. Rabbi Zalman Leib Gross's beard and peyos were shaved off; so were my peyos (I did not yet have a beard). He looked at me and said, "I don't think that you're really in pain." But he was. He was extremely wounded. The men would wear a kerchief around their faces until their beards grew back a little bit—the same sort of kerchief associated with toothaches. In our community, if you had a toothache, there was very little you could do about it except put a kerchief around your face and keep it warm, and maybe have a little schnapps. I remember that the rebbe of the community, whom I was close to, said to me, "Please don't look at me. I'm embarrassed." The idea of the beard, the rationale, was that it controls you, constrains you, disciplines you. With a beard, you wouldn't go to places you might otherwise go. I don't know what kind of extra discipline these men needed there, what their beards and peyos were keeping them from doing, what they would have done otherwise. But they were deeply wounded. And I could see their pain, their ache, their suffering. They felt opened up, unprotected.

Jewish law indicates what means may be used to cut the beard. For instance, one is not allowed to use a razor. According to some, even other kinds of shaving that are similar to using a razor are forbidden. But there is little discussion in the sources about having the beard itself. The assumption is that you do not have to have a beard as long as you remove it in the proper way. But kabbalistic literature emphasizes the positive aspects of having a beard. I, who looked at the Kabbalah mainly as poetry—beautiful, sometimes majestic, but not legally binding—had no religious problems shaving off my peyos. Indeed, I felt a sense of liberation. It made me look more like the outside world and made me feel freer. It gave me, or so I thought, a better chance of going out into the world and acquiring secular knowledge.

To the older people, a beard was a sign of identification, and they saw the Kabbalah as binding. A beard was something they had inherited from their ancestors, and taking it off was a catastrophe. It was taking away all their defenses.

There is a tradition that says the glory of the face is in the beard, and that only when a man has a full beard is he worthy of becoming a cantor or a leader of his people.

To those with this attitude, the order to shave off their beards was tantamount to taking away their dignity, their presence.

I SAID earlier that my formal education had ended when I was nine years old. Not quite. For almost to the very end—that is, almost to the deportation—a group of four or five young men met in the home of the Berbester Rav —this same Rabbi Zalman Leib Gross—to study practical law. Rabbi Zalman Leib Gross was a *dayan* in Sighet whose function it was to answer questions raised by the local Jews in their day-to-day life. Hours were set aside when the townspeople could come and ask questions pertaining to the whole gamut of religious observance, from how to prepare a kosher chicken to how to resolve business litigations (the latter when all the *dayanim* were present together). The answers to these questions are derived from the authoritative code of law, the *Shulchan Aruch*, composed in the sixteenth century by Rabbi Joseph Karo, and from the numerous commentaries accumulated since then. These rulings occupy seven large folio volumes divided into four orders. As future rabbis, we were supposed to know this material well, almost by heart. In these visits with the Berbester Rav we covered most of these volumes in the course of six or seven years.

A few times, Rabbi Zalman Leib Gross invited me to be present when the questions were asked, and once in a while he even asked my opinion. I remember an occasion when he chided me for my behavior in this forum. A woman came and, fearing the worst, asked in a tone of resignation what to do with a chicken that she had forgotten to singe before opening it up. Might she eat it? I burst into laughter. The scorching had nothing to do with religious requirements. It was done to get rid of the tiny feathers that remained after the chicken had been plucked. The Berbester Rav gave me a look. He told the woman very earnestly that the chicken was kosher, and when she left he took me to task for having laughed at her. "Your behavior," he said, "will discourage her in the future from asking a serious question."

After the war broke out we used to hear a summary of a radio broadcast in the morning, before we began our study sessions. Jews were not allowed to listen to foreign broadcasts, but some people defied the ban and shared the news with others. Among the listeners was the household of one of the young men in our group, the Berbester Rav's nephew. He would summarize for us the content of the broadcast and explain it. We treated his report as if it were a Talmudic text. We studied it meticulously, interpreted it, and drew all kinds of hypothetical conclusions. In our discussions of the news report the Berbester Rav was always inclined to the more pessimistic interpretation. He saw black when I thought that white, or at least less black, seemed equally plausible. He often repeated, "When a person is a murderer, the state will arrest and punish him; but when the state is the murderer, who will arrest and punish it?" One day, a few months before deportation, pessimism overcame him and he announced that the following semester we would study that portion of the code which deals with the problem of *agunot*, women who cannot remarry because it is not known whether their husbands are alive or dead (*Even Haezer*, chapter 17). "There will be," the Berbester Rav intoned with tears welling in his eyes, "many men who will not return home. They will be killed by the Nazis, but the circumstances of their death will not be known, with the result that their wives will be agunot, unable to remarry. We must ready ourselves now to prepare solutions to their problems so that these women do not remain forever 'living widows.' ''

Little did the Berbester Rav know that not only the men would not return. The women, too, would be murdered, and in larger numbers. They would be devoured in the crematoria because they were mothers. And the rabbis who so caringly worried about their remarriage would also not return. They all perished in the whirlwind of destruction.

IF I didn't go out much in the streets and didn't observe the events that engulfed the ghetto as a whole, I very pointedly observed the people around me. The shtiebel where I prayed was just across the street. I saw enough of my neighbors, family, and friends to realize the contrast: that while I did not find life in the ghetto unbearable or frightening, others did. I was not in trembling fear of immediate death, despite the objective facts all around me. I preferred not to see them and to continue doing what I was doing, which was possible only because of the ghetto's very short duration.

On the other hand, I did notice certain behavior which confused and perplexed me, which indicated that the optimistic view that prevailed—that we were not about to be killed, that we were going to work for Germany—was a façade. Deep down, the people around me did not believe it. I saw this in two things: one a trivial, almost amusing episode, and the other a more somber phenomenon.

In the ghetto, I was very much surprised that they let me have what they called *angemachts*. Before the Germans occupied Hungary in March of 1944, during the appropriate season families made preserves out of all kinds of fruits—a kind of syrup or jelly made of berries, prunes, and so on, and sugar. These preserves were kept in the house, high on a shelf, and were used only when a very important guest came—such as Grandfather's nephew Rabbi Hertzel Weiss, who was a well-known Talmud scholar—or when people were seriously sick and couldn't eat any other food. Then their families would tempt them with angemachts. As a child, I knew of two acts that indicated that a person was seriously sick. One was the family's calling in a second doctor. There were not that many doctors in Sighet, and if the first doctor was not alarming, a second one was not usually called. If a family called another doctor, it was only to make him contradict the previous doctor, whose diagnosis had been bad. The second ominous act was giving the sick person angemachts to eat. That they let me have the angemachts in the ghetto hinted to me that there was no future, nothing to preserve, nothing to keep, nothing to hold on to for the time to come. There was only a present that would soon evaporate.

But above all, I saw a clear indication that something was basically wrong with the belief that we would all survive this crisis in the way the ghetto people mourned the dead, and in their relationship with death. I was too sensitive not to see that the sorrow that went around the ghetto when a person died was not so horrendous, was

not so consuming, or deep, or penetrating. When somebody died in the ghetto—and I remember that my Great-
aunt Sarah Festinger died the day before we were
transported—people felt a sense of relief. I couldn't very
well reconcile this with the notion that we were just going
away temporarily to work and would ultimately return,
uncomfortable though the work might be. If that were all,
then death should have been just as sorrowful and un-
merciful as it was before. But it was not.

Funerals are the most expressive of class distinctions.
If you want to know how a community values its members, observe what kind of funeral it gives them. You can
see the social distinctions in the number and kind of people who attend the funeral procession and in both the content and the length of the speeches that accompany the
eulogy. Before the ghetto, we lived close to a cemetery—
our street led to a small street that in turn led to the
cemetery—which meant that every funeral had to pass
where I could see the funeral procession, at first from a
distance, then closer up, if I was outside on my own street.
I saw how people were treated. Even if I didn't know
whose funeral it was, I could surmise what kind of social
status the person had enjoyed while he or she was alive
from the goings on on the road to the cemetery. When a
prominent member died, the whole community participated, whereas when a member without high standing
died, the people who followed the coffin consisted exclusively of immediate family members and also, of course,
a representative of the burial society, the *chevra kadisha*.

The class distinction extended even into the cemetery
itself. In Sighet, and in many other places, some people
were buried in the choicer burial places, and others were

buried near the fence, which even in the time of the Talmud was considered a less important grave site. The less important, or less religious, or religiously problematic people were buried there. In the heart of the cemetery were the dignitaries; and in the case of chasidic rebbes, they were buried in an *ohel*, a kind of building made of stone and bricks, a semi-room, so their followers could come to pray there on the anniversary of their death and put in *kvitlach*, written wishes on small pieces of paper. Chasidic rebbes who didn't enjoy quite the same standing also had *ohalim*, dwellings or huts, but they were not built of stone and bricks. The less valued chasidic leaders were buried in wooden ohalim, and I remember how it always annoyed me that when Grandfather's wife died in the mid-thirties and a tombstone was erected with both of my grandparents' names, it was placed near the ohel of Rebbe Avigdor, belonging to a secondary group of chasidic rebbes whose graves had only a wooden shelter. It annoyed me that even there Grandfather, an acknowledged scholar, did not receive his due. Ultimately, of course, it did not make a difference; he died in Auschwitz. But it was symbolic, and if you were ever to visit the cemetery you would see that because he was not a descendant of a chasidic rebbe, Grandfather was not destined to be buried in an ohel, and his standing was not commensurate with his knowledge and scholarship.

On the same little street that led to the cemetery there was a slaughterhouse for fowl, which I used to frequent every week to get chicken for *Shabbos* from the *shochet*, Reb Menyu Rubin. I was struck by the fact that sometimes after a goose or a turkey was slaughtered and the esophagus pushed out, the bird still walked around for a while.

It looked as if it were still alive, and then it suddenly collapsed. There is even a Yiddish expression: "He walks around like a *geshochtene ganz*," like a slaughtered goose. Now, in the ghetto, I could not resist thinking, especially given the close proximity of the cemetery to the slaughterhouse, that our situation was not unlike that of the slaughtered goose. We were still walking, but it would not be for long.

In the ghetto, all funerals were the same, or so it looked from the outside. The cemetery was outside the ghetto and only very few people attended a funeral, almost always only a member or two of the family, a representative of the chevra kadisha, and the gravedigger. (He would have been a Jew, for I doubt that they allowed non-Jews to dig graves for Jews.) So it was, in a sense, a leveling experience. Even when Shiya Maggid died, a distant relative who was a rich and prominent member of the community, there was not much of a to-do. The funeral was simple and equal to that of any other person who died in the ghetto.

To repeat what I said before, what made me realize that there was more going on than what people said was that the people in the ghetto did not display the intense mourning or pain when somebody died that I remembered seeing when somebody died before the ghetto. In the ghetto, the mourning seemed to be much lower-key. In fact, it seemed even to be accompanied with a tinge of envy. I think this stemmed from the fact that the people in the ghetto wanted to be sure of having a Jewish burial and of being buried among Jews—of having a *Kever Yisrael*. It is a very important element of Jewish ritual that when the soul leaves the body ten Jewish people should be present and appropriate prayers should be said. The ritual ensures future resurrection and a share in the world to come, and the thought of it makes death easier.

IN THEIR wildest imagination, the people of the ghetto could not have imagined what ultimately happened. It could not have occurred to them that they would be gassed, that people, including young children, would be lured into a so-called delousing room, into a decent, respectable-looking room, even told to fold their clothes—all in order to deceive them—then would be driven in, forced in with truncheons, to a small vestibule that led to a big hall where they were later killed by gas. Many of them were probably killed before the gas was administered; they were simply crushed by the weight of the masses. Nor could the people of the ghetto have contemplated the possibility that they would not be buried at all. Instead, their remains were shoved into ovens and turned into ashes, and the bones that could not be burned were ground up and scattered into ponds and pits. All of this was beyond the range of their conscious imagination.

I believe that the people in the ghetto could imagine only two types of death at the hands of the Germans: starvation and being shot. Even though people did not die of starvation in Sighet, they suffered from it, and they knew what to anticipate. As far as being shot, I did not see any shooting in the ghetto, but people knew about it from the war. Basically, they were afraid, although they didn't say so, to die of shooting or starvation away from home, where they might not be buried among other Jews.

The fear that they might not be buried among Jews

indicated to me that the danger was real, that the optimistic talk was only a veneer, and that they were very much afraid about whether they would survive, whether they would come back from wherever they were taken.

THE PEOPLE of the ghetto tried desperately to suppress the signs of an imminent catastrophe the like of which is unknown in the bloody history of mankind. The signs were all around them, clear and poignant, but they refused to see them or acknowledge them. They suppressed these warnings but could not eradicate them. These signs entered their subconscious, generating fearful premonitions of the worst kind. It was these premonitions, this inarticulate dread, ineffable angst, which made life in the ghetto so torturous, so core-shaking, and which gave to ghetto life such an eerie, dreamlike quality. Whoever participated in that life, even for a short time, became a wounded relic of human cruelty, a creature of a blemished universe. The people of the ghetto are no more. But their fear and anguish persist, and will plague humankind until the end of days.

3

DURING
The Story of a Bletl

*When the Holy One, blessed be He, calls to mind
His children who are plunged in suffering among
the nations of the world, He lets fall two tears
into the ocean and the sound is heard from one end
of the world to the other—and that is the rumbling
of the earth [the earthquake].*
　　　　—*Babylonian Talmud*, Berakhot 59a

To the best of my knowledge, seismologists recorded
no disturbances in the vicinity of Sighet on March
19, 1944. But if earthquakes are caused by the sufferings
of Jews at the hands of other nations, then there ought to
have been dreadful tremors on that beautiful, crisp, early
spring morning when a neighbor knocked at our door,
telling us that the Germans had occupied Hungary. We
depended on this neighbor for news, because she had a
radio and we could not afford one. I closed the *Gemara*,
the Talmud I was learning, and I did not open it again

until the end of 1945. We were anxious to listen to the
developments, which were unfolding at a dizzying speed.
It also happened to be a few weeks before Passover, and
we had to think about preparing for the holiday. We knew
that under the Germans we would have difficulty procur-
ing Passover products. The rabbis were asked to give us
permission to eat beans, which normally are not eaten by
Ashkenazic Jews at Passover. After Passover we were
taken to the ghetto; later, to Auschwitz. That was on May
15, 1944. Soon after—I don't remember how many days,
perhaps a week—I was taken from Auschwitz and found
myself in one of the camps in Gross-Rosen, which is in
Lower Silesia. This was a few days before Shavuoth, the
holiday of Pentecost that follows seven weeks after Passover. In Gross-Rosen, I belonged to the sub-camp of
Wolfsberg, which had been built just a year or two before,
and which was now filled with Hungarian Jews, together
with some Polish Jews who came on the last transport
from the Lodz ghetto. Incidentally, one of the Lodz Jews
who was originally from Cracow, and who was a relation
of the Gerrer Rebbe, somehow managed to bring with him
a set of *tephilin* (phylacteries). Because of him, we had a
pair of tephilin in the camp.

EVENTS MOVED rapidly, one event pursuing another. I
had no time to reflect upon my plight. I had been taken
out of the kloiz to cut stones needed for building roads,
while my half-naked body was exposed to the sun. Somehow, I did not feel the enormity of my lot. Life was mere
survival, and because every day brought something new
or unpredictable, there was no time to consider my exis-

tential situation. In the course of time, life somehow settled into a routine. We used to get up when it was still
dark, work all day, and come back when it was already
dark. We had very little time for rest. That was, in a sense,
a blessing, for it prevented us from thinking about what
had happened to us, what was happening to us, and
what might be happening to our families. The thought
that my family would be totally destroyed—that of Grandfather's sixty-four children, grandchildren, and great-
grandchildren but five would survive—that thought did
not enter my mind. I cherished the thought that if I ever
survived and came home to my family and told them
about my experience, they would not believe me. So I used
to prepare in my mind some kind of proof to convince
them that I actually had experienced what I was relating
to them, that I was not exaggerating.

As I said, life somewhat settled down. Every second
Sunday was off, in official theory, but the Germans always
took us individually to do all kinds of work for which we
had to "volunteer." Nevertheless, on those rare Sundays
when we were not "volunteered" to work, we had a
chance to sit and talk to other Jews. As Jews usually do,
we learned, and because most of those who participated
in the learning were familiar with Tractate *Shabbat* of the
Mishnah, we chose to study that tractate. Familiarity with
Tractate *Shabbat* stems from its inclusion in the *siddur*,
the prayer book, which divides the tractate into three sections corresponding to the three Sabbath meals. Before
each meal one section is recited. I taught the mishnah of
Shabbat and others responded, commensurate with their
knowledge. When I myself did not remember a word or
two, there were always other rabbis who filled in. To-

gether we spent a few hours learning Mishnah on those rare second Sundays when we were off from work. Those were also the days when we were able to put on the phylacteries. All other days, we left when it was still dark, before it is permitted to put on phylacteries, and returned when it was already dark, when one may no longer put them on.

ONCE, TEACHING Mishnah, I was observed by a kapo, also called Weiss, whose workers were used as slave labor by a German company called Ackerman that was constructing underground tunnels to protect the soon-to-be-built munition factories from being bombed by the Allies. Jewish workers entered a tunnel only after it was dynamited to remove the stones. The actual dynamiting was not entrusted to Jews, to *Häftlinge*, prisoners of the camp, but was done at that time by Italians. Germany had occupied parts of Italy and, after the Italian armistice with the Allies in September 1943, sent some Italians to German concentration camps. They were treated better than the Jews, and they were the ones in charge of the dynamite. They dynamited the stony mountain and waited outside approximately half an hour, to make sure it was safe to enter. Then the Jews came in with the *chilas* to remove the dynamited stones. A chila (possibly from the Hungarian *csilla*) was a wagon on which they used to load and unload stones. The task of the Jewish workers was to enter the tunnel after the explosion, load the stones on the chilas, take them out of the tunnel, and unload them. The empty chilas were then returned to the tunnel and the process repeated. With each trip, the tunnel grew larger and so did the distance the chilas had to travel.

Let me add, parenthetically, that the Italians behaved extremely nicely. They kept on asking me what I had done wrong that I was sent to a concentration camp at the young age of fifteen. Somehow, the idea that Jews were taken to concentration camps en masse did not occur to them. Before Christmas 1944, they gave me a piece of bacon as a sign of sympathy and solidarity. I sold it for bread.

The Italians worked on an elevated platform from which they pinpointed the hole where the dynamite was to be placed. The platform was reached by a ladder. And if I finished before the regular work was completed, the Italians lifted me up to the platform, told me to rest, and pulled up the ladder. This prevented the Germans from climbing up and finding me there idle.

All of Ackerman's laborers worked very hard, even by concentration camp standards. Their shifts, however, consisted of only eight to ten hours, in contrast to the rest of the camp, whose shifts consisted of twelve hours. Because of their hard work, they enjoyed certain privileges and received additional provisions. They were given cigarettes, which some people exchanged for food. The Italians needed an abundant supply of drills to drill holes in which to place the dynamite. The drills became dull very quickly, and it was impossible to sharpen them inside the tunnel because of the hazard of using fire there. A smithy was placed right outside the tunnel to provide sharp drills. Jews were not trusted with fire. The smithy was manned by some not-so-pure Germans, and they needed somebody to go in and out of the tunnel to take the sharp drills to the Italians and bring back the dull drills. The one who was entrusted with this task had an easy job. If I remember correctly, a load consisted of five drills, which were not overly difficult to carry.

The kapo Weiss, who wasn't the kindest of kapos but was nevertheless taken by my teaching Mishnah, transferred me to Ackerman. Being so young, I was immediately assigned the job of carrying the drills into and out of the tunnel. That entitled me to all the privileges, benefits, and bonuses that those doing heavier work received.

This was not the only time my learning endeared me to a kapo. Another, by the name of Lefkowitz, who told me he was a former Gerrer chasid, always pumped me for the erotic parts of the Talmud and wanted me to recite them to him; but once he also saved me from a selection, which probably would have meant death.

After I was transferred to Ackerman, I had more time and was less fearful of the unexpected. My work settled into a routine and I was no longer under the constant surveillance of the Germans, as I had been before when I worked for another company, named Huta. Huta, my wife informs me, constructed the Auschwitz crematoria. There, if I stopped working, I had to keep the shovel in my hand while making sure, by looking at the SS guard, that his eyes didn't catch me not working. Had that happened, needless to say, I would have been in great trouble. At Ackerman I was almost—if I may use the word—independent. I saw to it that the Italians had enough sharp drills, and the rest was sort of my own time.

My job was to go into the tunnel—by now it was already more than a kilometer long—take the dull drills from the Italians, carry them out to the smithy, have them sharpened, and return them to the Italians. On an average night, I completed the route five or six times. The coming and going became routine and would have allowed my thoughts to wander, if not for something that was a matter of life and death: the chilas loaded with large stones. The passage through the tunnel was very narrow; there was hardly room for a person and a loaded chila to pass each other. Occasional niches in the wall were carved out to allow a person and a chila to pass. To facilitate the removal of the loaded chila, the path of the tunnel sloped down toward the outside so that the chila rolled out almost by itself. In order to stop it from rolling downward, the chila needed to be braked, and the brake was a simple wooden stick, which didn't always work. When the brake failed, anyone who was walking in the tunnel where there was no niche was sure to be killed. Also, each chila was accompanied by three people, needed for the loading and unloading. If the chila went too fast and the wooden brake did not work, the chila skidded, overturned, and killed the people accompanying it. Almost every day there were fatalities.

While walking into and out of the tunnel, each time I passed a niche I had to calculate when the chila would come by and, if necessary, wait for it there. I had an understanding with the people who accompanied the chila that they would shout, whistle, or communicate in some other way to notify me of their coming. Once I had convinced myself that I was not heading for a collision with the chila, I could have a quiet night, absorbed in my thoughts. For the first time since I had been torn from my home I had leisure to consider the possibility that things might not turn out as I had thought they would, that there might be no survivors, nobody to return to. While I walked through the tunnel carrying the drills, I could also think for the first time about learning. I particularly remembered the last letter I had written before the deportation, to a Hungarian rabbi by the name of Roth. He surely did not survive, but some of his children might have. The letter was a discussion, a typical Hungarian *pilpul* about Eliezer, the slave of Abraham, who was sent by his master to find a wife for Isaac. The question was whether Eliezer was merely a *shaliach l'shiduchin*, a messenger sent only to choose a wife for Isaac, with the actual betrothal to be done by Isaac himself; or a *shaliach l'kidushin*, authorized to actually betroth the bride on behalf of Isaac. The practical difference, of course, would have arisen in the event that Eliezer died before returning home. If he had been sent merely to choose a wife without betrothal, then Isaac's status would remain unchanged. If, however, he had been sent to actually betroth a wife for Isaac, and then died before Isaac was informed of his bride's identity, Isaac would be prohibited from marrying any woman at all, because she might be related to the one whom the messenger betrothed on his behalf. It was a diverting, almost amusing question, the kind of thought that comes easily to a traditional Talmudist. We had no text, nothing to look up. We depended on memory. Indulging in this kind of discussion was delightful; it brought a smile to the face.

Fifty years later, I am far from that kind of learning, but at that time remembering it was almost like meeting an old neighbor, a relative, or a friend. The text, the thought, made the connection with home. The more abstract, the more abstruse, the more bizarre the question, the more satisfying and contenting it was. It was so different from the environment in which I now found myself, so discordant with the style of life I was living, that it was like a greeting from a bygone age.

I HAVE not mentioned that, of course, the Germans were guarding the tunnel. At intervals, a German sentry was placed to see that everything in the tunnel was in order. In my journeys in and out, I met the sentries and, as camp protocol required, lifted my *mutze*, my cap, and greeted them. That became habit; I did it almost unconsciously.

Once I met a particular German who, I recognized, was not really a German, not a member of the SS, but a member of the Todt, the brigade founded by Fritz Todt, Hitler's chief civil engineer, which was in charge of construction work in Germany. I realized he was not a real German because his German was not very good. He avoided speaking it and used it only when he cursed and threatened. Otherwise, he didn't speak much. He was stationed at a crossroads in the tunnel so that he could see what was happening on all sides. I used to see him several times a night. If I went in and out of the tunnel five times during an eight- or ten-hour shift, I met him ten times. Each time I lifted my mutze and murmured my greetings. In the course of time, some sort of relationship developed between us, even though we never talked. Our eyes met and a kind of body language emerged. After several months, we knew each other in a peculiar way; we tolerated each other. One night, while I was walking the route, absorbed in my thoughts, with the false sense of security that routine provides—I still had to make sure the chila wouldn't bury me—I passed by the Todt as he was eating his scheduled snack, his meal between meals. In characteristic German style, he ate at the same time every night and, what's more, he ate the same thing every night: a thinly sliced sandwich containing some greasy substance that stained the wrapping paper and made it transparent. He and his eating habits became as much a feature of the tunnel as the chila and carrying the drills.

This time, however, our meeting was different. His sandwich was wrapped in a page of *Orach Chaim*, a volume of the *Shulchan Aruch*, Pesil Balaban's edition. The Balabans began publishing the *Shulchan Aruch*, the Jewish Code of Law, in Lemberg in 1839. The first publisher was Abraham Balaban, and after his death he was succeeded by his widow, Pesil. Pesil's edition of the *Shulchan Aruch* was the best; it had all the commentaries, including that of Rabbi Shloma Kluger. As a child of a poor but scholarly home, I had always wanted to have her edition. We had a *Shulchan Aruch*, but it wasn't Pesil's. Ours was also old and torn. It was my ambition as a child to own a *Vilner Shas* (a complete set of all the Talmud's volumes), Pesil's *Shulchan Aruch*, and a set of "*Rambams*," a complete set of Maimonides' major legal writings. Here, of all places, in the shadows of the tunnel, under the threatening gaze of the German, a page of the *Shulchan Aruch*, with fatty spots all over it, met my eyes. The page was from the laws of Passover (*Orach Chaim* 434). The question on the page deals with whether an agent can nullify the leavened bread of a household before Passover, which is the subject of a disagreement. On the one hand, why not? After all, isn't there a general rule: "A man's agent is like unto himself"—everything we can do a proxy can do for us? However, the *Ran*—a fourteenth-century scholar—argues that since *bittul* (the annulment) is a result of *hefker* (abandonment), the nullifying is considered a kind of disowning or dissolving of ownership, which cannot be done through an agent.

Upon seeing this wrapper, I instinctively fell at the feet of the guard, without even realizing why; the mere letters propelled me. With tears in my eyes, I implored him to give me this *bletl*, this page. For a while he didn't know what was happening; he thought I was suffering from epilepsy. He immediately put his hand to his revolver, the usual reaction to an unknown situation. But then he understood. This was, I explained to him, a page from a book I had studied at home. Please, I sobbed, give it to me as a souvenir. He gave me the bletl and I took it back to the camp. On the Sundays we had off, we now had not only Oral Torah but Written Torah as well. The bletl became a visible symbol of a connection between the camp and the activities of Jews throughout history. It was not important what the topic was, whether agency or any other. Perhaps it was symbolic; who knows what mission we were supposed to fulfill there? The bletl became a rallying point. We looked forward to studying it whenever we had free time, more so even than to the phylacteries. It was the bletl, parts of which had to be deciphered because the grease made some letters illegible, that summoned our attention. Most of those who came to listen didn't understand the subject matter, but that was irrelevant. They all perceived the symbolic significance of the bletl.

The bletl was entrusted to a Mr. Finkelstein—I believe

his name was Moshe—from Mátészalka, a town in Hungary where my father had been in the ghetto. Mr. Finkelstein was "a Jew who always prayed"; his lips always moved. I have a feeling that he wasn't sure after reciting his prayers once if he had recited them correctly. Or maybe he recited them once in the Ashkenazic pronunciation and once in the Sephardic. Having the bletl around in the camp was dangerous. Someone caught with it would be considered to be carrying contraband. Mr. Finkelstein volunteered to keep the bletl and, of course, produced it every second Sunday, when we were off. He must have carried it on his person; I'm sure he slept with it. The bletl was always with him and secure. Knowing that the bletl was with Mr. Finkelstein, we felt secure as well.

ALL THIS continued until February 1945, when we were transferred to Ebensee, part of the Mauthausen complex in Upper Austria, when the Gross-Rosen camp was liquidated and occupied by the Russians. In the last months of the Nazi demise Ebensee was the worst extermination camp anywhere in Germany or Austria. I remember having heard reports of cannibalism there. We were in a block—if I recall correctly, it was block 24—where the kapos were German criminals. The daily toll of dead, I believe, sometimes reached as high as eighty in our block alone. They used to pile up the sick and the weak on an arch near the windows, in the cold weather of March and April. By morning they were all dead. But even worse than that was the journey there. It took us from February until April to reach Ebensee from Gross-Rosen. Fewer than half of us survived. Life was unbearable; torture and death were everywhere; extermination was ubiquitous. In comparison with Ebensee, Ackerman was a paradise. There we worked; in Ebensee we collapsed. In Ebensee I was a mixer of cement, which was used for paving tunnels and other works. If I stopped turning the mixer for a moment, cement was not delivered and the whole work in the tunnel came to a standstill. I was at the end of my strength. At last I ran away and was caught. Fortunately, it was the day Hitler committed suicide, and the Yugoslavian kapo who was to administer the deadly lashes told me to shout, to feign having received the punishment.

I DIDN'T see Mr. Moshe Finkelstein in Ebensee, even though he was also there. I must confess that the bletl was not on my mind. The sheer need to survive under constant torture drove out any other interests. In Ebensee we didn't have second Sundays off; there was no possibility of learning. The episode of the bletl was blocked out of my memory. As the Talmud says, "Subsequent troubles cause the earlier ones to be forgotten." And troubles there were. Ebensee appeared like a bottomless inferno devouring all who entered it.

One day, while I was mixing cement in the big amphitheater—a kind of working plaza where chilas of all sizes and from all directions raced at me, this time to pick up cement—I spotted Mr. Finkelstein. He saw me as well. We tried to make contact, but it wasn't easy. We had to pass in front of kapos, each of whom had his own turf, which he guarded jealously against intruders. Finally, we made contact. He asked me whether I knew the prayer *vehikravtem* by heart. It was Passover, 1945. It was the first day of Chol Hamoed, the intermediate days of Passover, and he wanted to know the exact formulation of the sacrifices performed in the Temple service of old and recited in the *Musaf* prayer. Sacrifice was on Mr. Finkelstein's mind. How appropriate! He himself was a sacrifice; so were we all, lambs waiting for the slaughter. I told him the formulation and asked him about the bletl. He tapped his hip, and that was enough of a sign that, despite the horrible conditions, which killed perhaps as many as ninety percent of us, the bletl was safe and secure. We parted with a *"gut yom tov"* greeting.

Subsequently I heard from the Betlamer Rav that soon after we parted, Mr. Finkelstein collapsed. Before there was time to remove the bletl from his body, he was taken away to the crematorium. When Mr. Finkelstein's body went up in smoke, the bletl went with him.

4

LIBERATED
Life after the Holocaust

I was liberated on May 6, 1945, and came to America on February 11, 1947. During the intermediate year and a half, I first wandered in Germany for a few weeks, gathering strength to leave. I was almost too weak to move. After regaining some strength, I traveled by all possible means—by train (both inside and on the roof), by horse and buggy, and often on foot—to Sighet to see if any of my family had survived. None had. I spent a few days there, which coincided with the yearly nine days of mourning by Jews for the destruction of the First and Second Temples thousands of years ago, culminating in the fast of *Tisha B'Av.*

I remember fasting on Tisha B'Av, not out of sorrow for the destroyed Temples—more immediate sorrows compelled my commemoration—but out of a sense of historical continuity. Recent events had cruelly fractured that continuity, but I was trying desperately to hold on to it, to preserve contact with the past that had left me no living remnant and exposed me to abysmal loneliness.

FROM SIGHET I went to Budapest, staying there for a few months with a family whose father was from Sighet. Afterward I returned to Germany and joined a D.P. (displaced persons) camp with the intention of immigrating to America. In Budapest I began to acquire secular knowledge autodidactically, through reading newspapers and books in Hungarian. The family I was staying with was meticulously observant but, like the Orthodox in the West, was linguistically assimilated; its members thought and communicated in Hungarian. I began to read Hungarian (I retained some knowledge from the time I passed the first four elementary classes as an extern) and to speak it with an accent that gave rise to periodic laughter from some listeners. (Speakers of a language like Hungarian, which is not international but is spoken only by natives, are not accustomed to different accents and find any deviations from the accepted pronunciation comical.)

Knowing Hungarian served me as a conduit to the world at large, linking me to it and it to me. Not until much later, when I was already in the United States and read Yiddish literature assiduously, was my Yiddish adequate for more than conversational exchanges with the family and acquaintances and for the discussion of Talmud, which intermingles Hebrew words with Aramaic. All this time I still missed words, my Yiddish vocabulary was poor, and I was ignorant of its syntax. I could not express myself articulately even in Yiddish (though it was my mother tongue), and my writing in that language was sporadic. Hebrew was, of course, the holy language, reserved for reading sacred literature and cryptic writing. These limitations curtailed my contact with the non-Jewish world, with non-Yiddish speakers. Hungarian restored that contact, both orally and literarily. It provided me with a vehicle of communication. Not knowing that there was an English–Yiddish dictionary, I used Hungarian also to learn English, which I hoped would be my language of discourse when I arrived in America. As soon as I came to the States, I dropped Hungarian, and by now I have forgotten it almost entirely, not without some relief. For to this day, spoken Hungarian conjures up in my memory sounds I heard when we were deported from Sighet to Auschwitz—the brutality, the threats, the saber-rattling of the Hungarian gendarmerie. I have no desire to relive them.

The first time after liberation that I studied Talmud seriously, not just looking up references, was in Budapest in 1945–46, and it was disastrous. I was staying with the family I mentioned who knew me from Sighet. I am eternally grateful to them for taking me in so soon after liberation, while I was still suffering some of the physical symptoms incurred through camp life, and for serving me my first regular meal since Sighet. The family had succeeded in remaining in Budapest during the war relatively undisturbed, in their home and with their possessions, including a rich Judaic library. But with all their empathy and readiness to help, the difference in how we survived the war created a gulf between us. They continued to live in the style of prewar years, whereas I lived in the shadow of the cataclysm.

What united us most, offering a semblance of mutual

continuity, was the study of Talmud. Both the father and his son had studied with Grandfather. We all inherited something of Grandfather's uniqueness, which could serve as a common denominator. It was only natural that as soon as I joined their house, we scheduled a *shiur*, a study session of Talmud. I am sure they thought that the session would bring out our common intellectual background and also promote closer personal ties. What was not taken into consideration was that, to me, the study of Talmud was unalterably connected with a sense of security, of proving myself, of validating my worth. As soon as we began to study together, I had to show that I knew more than they: that they might have the worldly goods, the tranquillity, but I had the knowledge. I needed to prove that we were not that unequal after all. I had something they did not have, and taking me into their house was very possibly a privilege.

When they raised a question in the text, I had the answer most of the time, farfetched and forced, without having thought it out afresh or checking to see whether it fit. That was very different from Grandfather's style. He always pondered first, considering in his mind the different possibilities before he chose the right solution. My co-learners were taken by surprise. They did not expect this from me.

Moreover, in order to strengthen my argument, I used to shout (as if shouting would subdue my adversaries), which further disturbed my conservative co-learners, who insisted on decorum. The result was that after a few weeks the sessions were discontinued, under the pretext that something came up that did not allow time for study. I do not remember what tractate we studied. The content has totally slipped my mind—a further indication of how emotionally charged the endeavor must have been from the very beginning. Only the unpleasantness remained engraved in my memory.

WHILE I was in the D.P. camp I felt pressure to get married even though I was not yet fully eighteen—the optimal age, according to the famous statement in the Talmud's *Sayings of the Fathers*. The urge to build new families to replace the old, destroyed ones and to dispel loneliness was obviously the main factor in the plethora of marriages at that time. But it also took on the character of a religious compulsion, as it still does in the chasidic communities. Having decided that I wanted to go to school to pursue secular knowledge (and being fearful that I might not be able to support a family after the end of my stay in the D.P. camp), I did not want to be saddled with additional responsibilities.

When a rabbi I had known before (who later came to the States and wrote a well-known book about religious observance in Auschwitz about which I am quite skeptical) visited me in Munich around the middle of 1946 and offered me a choice of marrying either his niece or his daughter, I was prepared. I quoted for him a statement of the Talmud, said in the name of the sage Rabbi Meir (a second-century scholar of the land of Israel), that "a person shall first build a house [i.e., a livelihood] and only after that, marry a woman." The rabbi assuredly and authoritatively replied that Rabbi Meir's statement applied only when there were houses to build and when families existed. Having children could then be postponed. But in our generation, which treated Jewish children so cruelly, in which mothers were automatically gassed, getting married and having children as soon as possible was the first commandment, literally and figuratively. I did not dispute him. I could not. I told him that I would let him know, but did not. I could not bring myself to see him again and confront his trenchant arguments anew. I just let things drop. Subsequently, I learned that the rabbi himself had married the niece he had spoken about, who was about my age and half his own. (There was a shortage of women the rabbi's age or slightly younger. Before they were taken to Auschwitz they were mothers already, and Hitler claimed them all for the crematoria.) This rabbi and his young wife had many children and grandchildren.

I CAME to the United States on February 11, 1947, as part of a group of orphaned children under the age of eighteen—my papers were ready in Germany before I actually became eighteen—who were brought to this country for adoption under the auspices of Eleanor Roosevelt, who headed a committee for children found in the European theater of war. I remember that we arrived at midday and were taken to an orphanage on Caldwell Avenue in the Bronx, where they served us cold milk. I still savor the taste; after years of starvation, to be able to drink as much cold milk as one wanted was a memorable event. But then in the evening they served a dinner with meat, and the question of Jewish dietary laws came up. If I remember correctly, out of fifteen children, three ate kosher, and they followed my lead. They were in a precarious psychological state, and I worried about them. (One of these children, by the name of Rosenfeld, jumped to his death from a building a few months later.)

I wanted to make sure the meat was kosher, and the director obliged me by bringing in a young man who supervised the kitchen to see that it conformed to the dietary laws. The young man, I later found out, was from one of the right-wing *yeshivot*, *Torah VoDaath*, but he had no beard. It was the first time I had seen a rabbi without a beard, so naturally I had some hesitation about his supervision. Since I was very hungry and anxious to eat, as were the people following me, I tested him by asking him a question on the law. I was already ordained and asked him the kind of question I would have been asked in Sighet, an interpretation of a text that is part of a commentary on the *Shulchan Aruch*, which we had to study for ordination. The commentary was called *Peri Megadim*, and I subsequently learned that rabbinical students in the United States did not study it as intensively as we did in Europe.

I asked the young man the question and he did not know the answer. His not knowing made me doubt his reliability, and we did not eat. The incident proved to be embarrassing to the management. The place had a reputation for being strictly kosher and we, who had come from Europe, from concentration camps, did not want to eat there. We also had a problem of language. We couldn't talk to the orphanage staff because we did not know English well enough. Someone had the bright idea to bring in a social worker who could speak Yiddish to try to convince us to eat. They brought a social worker by the name of Shulamit Halkin, granddaughter of the *Netziv*, who also happened to be the sister-in-law of Professor Saul Lieberman, the scion of a famous scholarly family in Lithuania. She spoke a different Yiddish, Lithuanian Yiddish—I was more accustomed to Galician Yiddish. She addressed herself earnestly to me. But speaking Yiddish is no guarantee, no certificate of *kashrut*, of meeting the dietary requirements. We had to go to sleep without eating meat. But she had asked me, "If I take you to the person who I think is the greatest Talmud scholar, will you go?"

I said, "Of course I'll go."

The next morning, February 12, 1947, she took me to Professor Lieberman's home. I was enormously impressed by his erudition, which probably was unrivaled by that of any living scholar. Even when he didn't want to impress, he was impressive. This time he wanted to impress. He wanted to make sure that I would eat. He explained that the meat was kosher even though the fellow who supervised didn't know how to answer my question. After a few hours of discussion, he sent me back to the orphanage, where we stayed for a few more days and then were sent to another orphanage; and we ate, of course.

From this first, long discussion with Professor Lieberman that day, concerning Talmudic subjects, I remember only one *Tosafot*, a passage of medieval commentary on the Babylonian Talmud, on Tractate *Chulin* 97a, in which I had the upper hand because I remembered it better than he did. At the time he did not say anything. But as I left —when I was already at the door and turned back to thank him again—I noticed that he had taken out the *Chulin* folio of the Talmud, turned to the first page, and begun to study. I asked him "Why *Chulin*?" and he answered, "If I forgot one Tosafot, who knows how many others I may also have forgotten?" Erudition is a steady endeavor.

This first casual meeting with Professor Lieberman may have changed the course of my life. Given the perception of the Jewish Theological Seminary in yeshiva circles, I doubt very much that I would ever have gone to the Seminary had I not first met Professor Lieberman, and had I not been so impressed by his enormous scholarly capabilities and by what I took at the time to be a simple, almost naïve religiosity. Had I not eventually gone to the Seminary, I doubt very much if, despite my native inclination toward *peshat*—toward the simple meaning of texts unencumbered by tortuous interpretations—I would have developed into a full-fledged Talmud scholar, dedicated to the scientific, critical method.

As it was, the meeting with Professor Lieberman was a humbling experience as well, especially since I had then been out of the habit of learning for some time. But I had not been humble just a month before in Munich, where I acted as if I knew it all.

Before I came to the United States, I spent about eight months in a D.P. camp in Windsheim, not far from Fürth, in Bavaria. Toward the end of our stay there, children who planned to go to America were taken to a children's camp, to Prien near the Chiemsee, and during the last week or so before leaving were quarantined in Munich in the Funk Kaserne. From there we traveled to Bremerhaven and embarked on a ship to New York. During my stay in the Funk Kaserne, I petitioned the commander of the camp, an American, to allow me to go out to buy kosher food. He told me that if I brought him a letter from the rabbi of the town that I eat kosher, he would let me out. It sounded very reasonable, and without much ado I took the *Strassenbahn*—the streetcar—and shlepped myself to Romerstrasse (if I remember correctly, Romerstrasse 21), where the rabbinate was located. I knocked on the door of Rabbi Snieg and told him confidently and a bit arrogantly that I had come to ask him for a statement that I eat kosher. The rabbi looked at me and said, "This is the first time I see you. How do I know that you eat kosher?" I was flabbergasted and totally taken aback by this very logical question, which had not occurred to me. The rabbi must have noticed my embarrassment and, wanting to help, he asked in a friendly tone, "Have you ever studied something?" I understood right away that this cryptic sentence in Yiddish meant, had I ever studied Talmud, or at least the Pentateuch. If I learned "something" of the Talmud, or even of the Pentateuch, I probably ate kosher, though it was far from being a foolproof test.

I said, "Yes, I did study something."

"May I test you?" he asked. I said yes.

"On what material?" he continued.

"Whatever you want," I replied. He was taken aback by my audacious reply and said, "I will ask you about something I have been thinking about lately."

Again, the tone told me that he now considered me his colleague. He began: The Talmud discusses the question of whether identification marks, *simanim*, that a person gives in order to reclaim a lost object are legally valid biblically or valid merely by Rabbinic law. Are they reliable enough to permit a woman to remarry after she lost her divorce certificate and reclaimed it through identification marks? Why should this be a question? the rabbi inquired. In another place in the Talmud, the opinion is expressed that if one of two litigants is making a positive claim—one says, "You owe me money," and the other says, "I am not certain about it, I do not remember"— the latter has to pay. We believe the former litigant, "for where a positive plea is met by an uncertain one, the positive plea prevails."

Now, exclaimed the rabbi, why should we not apply the same principle to the lost object? The one who gives the identification marks is certain that this object is his or hers. The one who found it is uncertain to whom it belongs. According to the above principle, we should believe, according to biblical law, the one who makes the positive claim, the one who offers the marks.

I responded that the two cases are not the same. In the case of the loan, the litigation is limited to these two people. Nobody else is involved. Therefore, if one party is sure and the other party is not sure, we believe the one who is sure. But in the case of the lost object, although at present there are only two litigants, it is quite possible that in the future other people will come forth claiming equally positively that the object is theirs. We cannot release the lost object to the one who is now giving identification marks, for there may be others in the future who will do the same. I subsequently read a similar explanation in a book, but at that time it was new to me.

The rabbi wrote out a letter to the commander of the Funk Kaserne that I eat, and have always eaten, only kosher food and that he would appreciate any courtesy extended to me in this regard.

What made me so boastful as to challenge him to ask me a question on whatever subject he wanted was the utter shock, the unpreparedness, of not having anticipated the possibility that a man whom I had never seen would ask me such a question. I had shlepped along on the Strassenbahn for almost two hours from one end of town to the other without imagining the possibility of such a question. Otherwise, I am not given to such vanity.

A YEAR or so after I came to the United States, while I was in high school, I decided to Hebraize the name Weiss (White) to a biblical equivalent, Halivni (see Numbers 3:21, 26:58). I was always bothered by the German sound of the name Weiss, especially so after I learned that an SS officer by the name of Martin Weiss was the commandant of Majdanek, one of the six principal extermination camps, from September 1943 to May 1944. A Major Weis may well have been the first German commanding officer to order the killing of Jews in the occupied lands: a few days before the order came from higher command, on June 27, 1941, five days after the German invasion of Russia, he ordered his battalion police to murder Jews in Bialystok. Rumors also circulated that yet another SS officer killed Jews who bore family names resembling his own. But I did not have the heart to erase Grandfather's name. So now, when I write in English—not so in Hebrew—I keep both names, Weiss and Halivni, although I prefer to be addressed as Halivni only.

I BEGAN studying at Brooklyn College in 1949 while I was living in a yeshiva dormitory. I attended college during the day, combining yeshiva study with college study.

(Most yeshiva students at that time attended college only at night.) I insisted on attending during the day, and the yeshiva allowed me to do so. I was older than most high-school students entering college, and I did not want to delay graduation even longer by going at night.

Several attempts were made to dissuade me from going to college and encourage me to devote all my time to the study of Talmud, from appealing to my family's background ("What would your grandfather say to your wasting time in college?") to the future of the Jewish people ("Without Talmud scholars, the Jewish people will not survive!"). These attempts came from colleagues and from sources close to the yeshiva, and even from members of the family I stayed with in Budapest. The latter advised me against going to college not so much out of religious conviction as out of a deep-seated belief in the futility of formal education, which they did not pursue, paying a price for that omission when they later came to America.

I BELIEVE it is of historic interest for me to record here the conversations about going to college that I had with two of the foremost leaders of right-wing Judaism in America of the time—Rav Aaron Kotler, who more than anybody else transferred yeshiva learning and the yeshiva lifestyle to America, and the Satmarer Rebbe, Rabbi Joel Teitelbaum, who single-handedly restored Hungarian *chasidut* and community life. It was my good fortune to have been asked to accompany Rav Aaron Kotler, who lived at West Ninety-eighth Street in Manhattan, to a wedding in Brooklyn at Ninth Avenue and Forty-seventh Street. The trip lasted approximately three-quarters of an hour one way. We traveled by taxi. Rav Aaron stayed there only for the *chupah*, the ceremony, after which I accompanied him back to Manhattan.

I did not know Rav Kotler from before, and on the way there he asked me what I was doing. I told him that I was studying in the yeshiva, with which he had some connection. There was even talk of a merger between our yeshiva and his yeshiva in Lakewood, New Jersey.

There was nothing unusual about the trip. It was standard procedure for yeshiva students to accompany *rashei yeshivot*, their teachers, in cars to attend weddings. The conversation usually revolved around the subject matter that the *rosh yeshiva* had taught that week, or that the student had studied. I do not remember what we talked about on the way to the wedding. I only remember that Rav Kotler talked so fast and incessantly as to be difficult to understand at times, and that he gave me no chance to respond.

This changed on my way back. Apparently, somebody tipped him off that I was going to college and asked him to influence me to change my mind. On the way back, there was only one subject: the need to produce *talmidei chachamim*, Talmud scholars. This time Rav Kotler was clear and slow; he accentuated his words and waited for my reaction. I tried to divert his attention to something else, but to no avail. He hammered at the topic that studying Torah is more important than going to college, that the subjects taught in college are inferior in moral content, intellectual rigor, and elevation of spirit. But above all, he argued, there are plenty of people who go to college and so few people who go to yeshiva (at that time there really were not many). He derided the value of secular knowledge by minimizing its achievement.

I could not break out of what sounded to me like a harangue against secular study. I sat quietly and listened, until we passed through a tunnel—I believe it was the Brooklyn–Battery Tunnel, which had been built just a few years before. Rav Kotler stopped talking and looked out the window, to the right and to the left. He bent forward and strained his neck to look backward.

"All water," he said with excitement. "On the top water, below water, and on the side water!" I couldn't resist and said, "Reb Aaron, this is what they teach in college." Without a minute's hesitation, he retorted, "They have already tunnels."

At the time I considered his answer naïve in the extreme. Almost fifty years later, however, I find myself saying much the same thing, appealing to students, particularly female students, to take on graduate study in Talmud. I tell them, "There are plenty of doctors, lawyers, and engineers. One more doctor, lawyer, or engineer would not make much of a difference. But a woman *talmidath chacham*, a serious Talmud scholar, would be of historical significance and make quite a difference in the sociological balance between the sexes." It may not be so naïve when the shoe is on the other foot.

THE SATMARER Rebbe I knew from Europe. He was born in Sighet and came to Sighet every year on the yahrzeit of his father. When he came to town, Grandfather took me to him for a *farher*, to have me tested. In 1942, to the displeasure of Grandfather, who was a Belzer chasid, I spent the High Holy Days in Satmar, prayed in the rebbe's synagogue, and attended his *tish*, the communal meal with his chasidim. I did that, I remember, because I wanted to ingratiate myself with him so that he would support my candidacy when I applied for a rabbinic position. He controlled the positions in the region, and without his approval it would be almost impossible to obtain one. At the time, I was about fourteen and already preparing for ordination. Also, his wife was very friendly with a cousin of ours in Satmar, and I had seen his wife several times at the cousin's house.

When the Satmarer Rebbe came to New York in 1947, for a while his yeshiva received no official recognition from the state, and it was attached to our yeshiva, Yeshivat Rav Chaim Berlin, which was much larger and older. As a result, he got to know the head of our yeshiva, Rav Yitzhak Hutner. One day, Rav Hutner told me that the Satmarer Rebbe wanted to see me. I went to see him and he received me very cordially. We learned together (I remember that we discussed, among other things, the beginning of the first page of Tractate *Zevachim* in the Babylonian Talmud) and we reminisced. In the course of the conversation he said to me, "I hear you are going to school."

"Yes," I said.

"Why?" he continued.

"Because I would like to learn the language of the country." I thought this would be less offensive than telling him I was studying philosophy.

"But I hear that you are going not only to school [meaning high school] but also to [college]. Why?"

"Because if I am already doing something, I want to do it well," I said sheepishly. This brought a smile to his face. He apparently saw through me, realizing that I was not telling him the truth, because he then told a story of a certain rabbi's son who did not want his wife to wear a wig (required of all married women) "because"—and he giggled—"a wig is not genuine. It is neither the woman's own hair nor a real cover. It is interesting how readily people resort to perfection when it comes to not obeying the law."

But the atmosphere was pleasant and the conversation lasted for hours until the *rebetzin*, his wife, came in and motioned to him to tell her my identity. He told her who I was and she said, interrogatorily, "Where is his *biber* hat [the round hat that Satmarer chasidim wear]? Where are his peyos?" And the rebbe retorted sarcastically, "He became a *Litvak*"—he became one of the Lithuanian Jews who are religious but wear modern clothes.

MY LITHUANIAN "pedigree" was reconfirmed later when I was already at the Jewish Theological Seminary and on my way to joining the faculty. Professor Lieberman boasted to Dr. Louis Finkelstein, the chancellor of the Seminary, in my presence, that he had made a Litvak out of me. Lieberman being a veritable Litvak himself, I took this statement as a compliment, meaning that despite my Hungarian background I had adapted well to the scientific study of Talmud, which in his eyes was identical with the classical Lithuanian style of learning, tracing back to the Gaon of Vilna (1720–1797), shunning pilpul, the convoluted reasoning I had encountered in my youth.

Incidentally, although by dint of hometown I might be called an *Ungarisher*, a Hungarian Jew, my background is not properly called Hungarian but is, in fact, closer to Galician, both spiritually and ethnically. Most of the Jews in my region originally came from Galicia in Eastern Europe (divided between Poland and Ukraine), and their lifestyle was similar to that of the Jews there. Some of them even remained chasidim of Galician rebbes. Politically, however, the region was attached to Hungary from the sixteenth century to the First World War. After that war the region was split between Romania and Czechoslovakia. It was reacquired by the Hungarians in 1938–40. The section I was born in became Russian after the Second World War and now it is in the Ukraine. Because of its pre–First World War history, the region is often referred to by other Jews as Hungary when the reference is made in Yiddish or by people who were brought up on Yiddish. The reference is usually derogatory, though there is no agreement on the specific characteristics that it supposedly connotes. Some accuse the "Hungarians" of being naïve and gullible; others, of being shrewd and pushy. When I came to America, I lived in two orphanages; the second was in Tuckahoe, New York, not far from New York City. The rabbi there was a graduate of Yeshiva University and wanted me to go there. I was interviewed by Rabbi Gorelik, who assigned me to the class of Rabbi Zaks. When he introduced me to Rabbi Zaks, he prefaced his introduction by saying that I was an "Ungarisher." I do not think he meant it derogatorily, but at the time I took it that way. I did not go to Yeshiva University. Instead I went to Yeshivat Rav Chaim Berlin. (Years later, Yeshiva University's president, Dr. Samuel Belkin, was interested enough in having me join his faculty that he interviewed me.) When I told Rabbi Yitzhak Hutner about my introduction at Yeshiva University, he consoled me by saying, "Was not Moses introduced to his future father-in-law, Reuel, by none other than his wife-to-be, Tzipora? And did not she, among others, refer to him as an Egyptian?" (See Exodus 2:19.)

AT THE time I visited the Satmarer Rebbe he had very few chasidim. Few American Jews went to visit him; therefore my visit was welcome. It was before the laws against immigration from our region of Europe were relaxed. After these laws were changed, the number of his chasidim in America reached into the thousands, and I was not sure I would still be welcome. I did not try, and did not go. When I joined the Seminary I was convinced that all doors were now locked. They were, however, punctured by a call from one of his followers, who would not have made it without the rebbe's consent, and who wanted to take out an anti-Zionist book from the Seminary's library. I like to think that, aside from fierce anti-Zionism, knowing that one of them was "there" encouraged the chasid who made this call to bridge the distance.

Years later, I indirectly heard from a third cousin who had recently come from Rine, a village near Sighet, and visited the rebbe that the rebbe told him that he had yet another relative—me—and even though I was with "them" (I assume he meant I was at the Seminary among Conservative Jews), I was still "better" than many who called themselves Orthodox. (My cousin, newcomer that he was, did not understand what the rebbe meant.)

Whether it was a compliment to me or a dig at the Zionist Orthodox, we will never know.

In this connection, let me also mention that part of my dissertation in 1958 was an identification of the first three pages of the pseudo-Rashi on the Babylonian Talmud, Tractate *Ta'anit* (the commentary that takes the place of Rashi's eleventh-century commentary on the first three pages of this tractate). On the basis of literary comparison, I proved that these pages cannot be attributed to the author of the remaining comments on the tractate, but rather belong to the commentary of Rabbi Gershom of the tenth century. I found, in the Seminary's rare book collection, a manuscript of the entire commentary on *Ta'anit*, which had the original three pages. The result of this discovery was published soon afterward in *Sinai*, an Orthodox scholarly journal. Incidentally, the bulk of the article was composed in my mind during the wee hours of the morning while pacifying my firstborn baby son, Baruch, who was lying in his crib and crying in pain from earaches.

A few years later, somebody published (anonymously and without a date, but I surmised it was a Satmarer chasid) the commentary of a student of the fourteenth-century Rabbi Peretz of Corbeil, France, on Tractate *Ta'anit*. In this work, by way of commenting on the first three pages, the student of Rabbi Peretz quotes, in the name of Rashi, what I had found in the manuscript, which is absent in our printed edition. This further proved my thesis. The editor did not mention my studies, and I suspected that was because I was affiliated with the Seminary (a common snub). I sent away an angry letter to *Sinai* in which I added this proof and attacked and criticized those who would not use relevant material and scholarship because of objections to the religious views of the authors. When I continued reading the commentary, however, I realized that I owed the editor of the commentary of the student of Rabbi Peretz a public apology. He does quote me in his book, quite respectfully, in another context. What he did not see was an article in the Orthodox journal.

I suspected that because I come from the same geographical area as the Satmar chasidim, they might judge me more leniently. Or they might nevertheless be proud that one of "theirs" was doing well with "them."

EVEN THOUGH I was born among chasidim—literally in the Poljaner Rebbe's house—lived among chasidim (if there were *mitnagdim*, religious Jews who were not chasidim, in Sighet, I did not know them), and was exposed to constant telling and retelling by Grandfather of the wondrous deeds of the Belzer Rebbes (to distinguish a chasidic rabbi from a non-chasidic rabbi, I usually call the former "Rebbe," his title in the Yiddish vernacular), I was never a real chasid, even when I was living in Sighet. What I have retained from chasidut, to this day, is the enthusiasm and intensity of prayer. As far back as I can remember, I was distanced by the intellectual limitations of chasidim, at first mistakenly thinking that they, among religious Jews, were the only ones who opposed the study of secular subjects. Later, I met mitnagdim who were no less fiercely opposed to secular knowledge. But above all I had difficulty accepting the concept of the *Tzadik*—the leader, who is endowed with superhuman qualities that give him access to the divine not available to ordinary

93

mortals. The concept is a cornerstone of chasidut. I had difficulty, not so much in principle as in practice, finding people with such qualities.

When a chasid talks of his rebbe, he enters into an emotional state that inflames him with love and saturates him with empathy for his subject, making him see no faults or shortcomings. What he does see—always positive—takes on extraordinary proportions bordering on the supernatural. I was never privy to this type of emotional state, and what I saw was much more ordinary, and not always beyond reproach. With such vision I could not be a real chasid of a chasidic rebbe or of a mitnagdic *godel*, a great man—the difference, of late, is only external.

My reluctance to attribute superhuman qualities to the chasidic rebbes may also be partially responsible for my having adopted the critical method in my study of the Talmud. The critical method is less credulous of the present available text, finds fault with it, and looks for a more credible and accurate one. In history, the critical method is less trusting of what is said and may declare a statement or an interpretation unreliable, arguing (as I rarely do) that the uncertainty stems from the idiosyncratic nature or from the social and economic interest of the sage who said it. Critical scholarship does not suffer hagiography, for while it is willing to concede that the hero was a superior human being, it is not willing to declare him superhuman, free of faults and mistakes.

A chasid who believes that his rebbe possesses superhuman qualities will not employ the critical method. Criteria suited to ordinary humans and their creations are ill suited to superhumans and their creations.

Let us also remember that finding fault in others is, after all, the result of envy—something to which I am prone. The chasidic rebbes were affluent and we were poor. They were glorified and we, despite our learning, were downtrodden. Their physical life, in general, was much more pleasurable than ours. All of this may have infused me with envy (although if I had been a real chasid I would not have been envious) and may have impaired my judgment.

I may also have been prejudiced. Not having been born one of them (though I married into this class), I resented their holding on to their turf, guarding it ferociously against intrusion by the non-dynastic class. The prejudice may have refracted my vision to see negatives where there were really none. All this is decidedly a possibility, but not more than that.

TO BE fair, let me also state that some scholars are opposed to the method I have adopted. They consider it too subjective, too speculative. To be objective, scientifically sound, according to them, it would have to be based exclusively on explicit textual references, parallel sources and manuscripts, and not on logical deduction, which I am wont to employ as well. According to these scholars, one cannot infer the existence of antecedent texts through dialectical deductions. A text has to be seen before an assertion can be made about its existence. Otherwise, it is merely conjectural, scientifically inadmissible. Once a standard like this has been set up, there is really very little left for the textual scholar to do but to seek out and prepare new texts. True creative and imaginative scholarship becomes well-nigh impossible. One does not have to be especially creative or particularly imaginative to understand a text when one has read one. Such intellectual activity does not complement reality. It merely focuses on it. But one cannot understand the full significance of a text without transcending it, without reaching out into its evolutionary past. That only an intuitive grasp can yield such an understanding does not diminish its veracity. On the contrary, through such intuition the text—that is, the content of the text—becomes firmer, rooted, and hence more reliable. It is endowed with a richness, a mellowness, a depth that enhance its credibility. A text, like a human being, is true to itself only when it is more than itself.

It would not be irrelevant here to mention that my taste in painting is for Impressionism and early Post-Impressionism. Unlike classical painting, to which the reigning Talmud scholarship can be compared, for it strives toward an articulate, harmonious whole, and unlike modern painting, which decidedly emphasizes the disharmonious, Impressionism leaves it to the viewer to complete the harmony, soliciting intuitive human participation.

IN COLLEGE, I majored in philosophy. I chose philosophy, I thought, because it agreed with my general inclination toward abstract thinking. It is, however, also possible (and I was told so by a friend who disparaged my going to college) that I chose philosophy because, even where I came from, the Philosopher was renowned as the embodiment of wisdom in the secular world, the symbol of knowing all that is to be known, and so by becoming a philosopher, I was subconsciously transforming myself into a wizard of wisdom and knowledge. Be that as it may, I soon had another rationale. I would study philosophy and logic and apply it to Talmudic reasoning with the aim of showing that despite its seeming inchoateness, Talmudic reasoning is based on objective and sturdy logic. For that purpose, I selected *kal vachomer* (an inference from minor to major or from major to minor), which is the most logical of the thirteen hermeneutic principles of Rabbi Ishmael—an early-second-century scholar of the land of Israel—which governed Midrashic exegesis and subjected it to systematic rigor. From the most logical, I had hoped to proceed to the less logical, thus covering the whole Talmud. So obsessed was I with the subject that I must have buttonholed anybody and everybody who was a potential listener, with the result that when some of my colleagues at the yeshiva saw me at a distance, they used to ward me off by saying, "Today no kal vachomers." Gradually, however, I realized that Talmudic reasoning is not so much a matter of logic as it is a matter of history: the vicissitudes of history, more than logical consistency, determined the reasoning. My enthusiasm for combining the two, philosophy and Talmud, was dampened. I abandoned kal vachomer studies after salvaging a few formulas which I developed and which I still use today, and returned to straight philosophy. I still enjoyed philosophy and I studied it for its own sake, but I was searching for a philosophy "of" something. I chose the philosophy of religion. I wrote a master's thesis on the theology of the Protestant theologian Paul Tillich, comparing his ideas to parallels in Judaism. This brought me back home to the study of Jewish sources, which, soon after I left the uni-

versity, I pursued at the Jewish Theological Seminary—
where Professor Lieberman, pure philologist that he was
(at least, that is how he saw himself), discouraged my interest in philosophy, and I concentrated on textual studies.

DESPITE MY connection with Professor Lieberman and
casual acquaintance with some other faculty members, my
entering the Seminary was not without tension. For one
thing, it had the appearance of a downtown Brooklynite
(my yeshiva was on Stone Avenue in Brooklyn) moving to
uptown Manhattan, which in previous generations meant
an Orthodox East European Jew pushing himself to be
accepted among the *yehudim*, the non-Orthodox Jews of
German extraction.

But that picture of the Seminary was utterly false.
When I came to the Seminary at the beginning of 1954,
there was not a single teacher who had been born in Western Europe, and almost all the teachers had studied at
some sort of yeshiva. Nevertheless, the myth in the yeshiva
was that the Seminary was both religiously and emotionally "Germanic"—lax in observance and stiff in emotional
response: qualities that made me fear I would not be comfortable there. The fear proved to be totally unwarranted.

At the Seminary, I was struck by the mixture of yeshiva
and university. In the Talmud class, the atmosphere was
closer to the discipline of the yeshivot than to the free-
wheeling American universities. The roles of teacher and
student were clearly delineated: the teacher was a dis-
penser of knowledge, the student a listener and receiver.
These roles rarely overlapped. In the nontextual classes,
the atmosphere was different; the roles sometimes inter-

mingled. I remember during my first week at the Seminary, in a homiletics class, the teacher cited the famous Talmudic parable of "a human king who owned a beautiful orchard which contained splendid figs. He appointed two watchmen, one lame and the other blind. One day the lame man said to the blind man, 'I see beautiful figs in the orchard. Come and take me upon your shoulders so that we may procure and eat them.' When the owner of the orchard came and inquired, 'Where are the beautiful figs?' the lame man replied, 'Have I feet to walk with?' The blind man replied, 'Have I eyes to see with?' What did the king do? He placed the lame man upon the blind man and judged them together. So, too, the Holy One, blessed be He, will take the soul, place it in the body, and judge them together" (Babylonian Talmud, *Sanhedrin* 91b). A student raised his hand and asked the teacher for the source of this parable. The teacher replied, "I do not know. Perhaps Mr. Weiss knows." I did not expect the teacher to know my background. But what amazed me most was that I was totally unprepared for a teacher to confess publicly that he did not know a source in the Talmud and to ask a freshman to enlighten him. Even though I knew the source, I feigned ignorance. I could not overcome my inner reluctance to blur the distinctive roles of the teacher and the student.

IN THE beginning I also had objective reasons to worry whether I would be accepted altogether. Because of a scholarly program that had gone sour just a few years before I applied, the Seminary offered only the rabbinic track, not the Ph.D. program that interested me, and I was advised by everyone to say that I wanted to become a pulpit rabbi. However, when one of the interviewers (who later became a close friend) asked me a standard question—"Which Conservative rabbi inspired you to take on this calling?"—I could not name a single Conservative rabbi who had a synagogue. The interviewers began to suspect that I was not telling the truth, that I had ulterior motives. Some of them, I heard later, were inclined to reject me. They had not had much *nachas*, much satisfaction, from survivors who became students. Of those who took pulpits, few could be counted successful. Often the Americanization of the congregations remained an insurmountable obstacle for rabbis with European suffering in their backgrounds. My interviewers were not inclined to risk one more such student, especially one not fully forthcoming with the truth. This was one of several situations I encountered in which people with the best of intentions did not know how to treat us survivors and, because of our background, had low expectations of us.

What exactly happened afterward I do not know, but a few days later I received a letter from the chancellor, Dr. Louis Finkelstein, saying that he wanted to see me. That meant, an older Seminary student erroneously informed me, that I had been rejected. The admissions committee did not want to tell applicants directly because they knew some of them personally. They therefore asked the chancellor to sugar-coat the notification. I felt upset and wondered whether the leaders of the yeshiva had heard of my debacle at the Seminary and whether I would still be able to return there. It was soon after my marriage, so I was especially concerned about my future. When I met Dr. Finkelstein, I concluded that I had nothing to lose, and when he asked me why I wanted to come to the Seminary, I told him the truth: "To study *Yerushalmi* [the Jerusalem Talmud] with Professor Lieberman." That "saved the situation" (a favorite phrase of Dr. Finkelstein's), and it fit my image and what he had heard about me from Professor Lieberman. A few days later, I received a letter of acceptance.

Had I said that I wanted to be a pulpit rabbi, Dr. Finkelstein would have rejected me, too. Somehow, the interviewers were convinced that I was not suitable for the congregational rabbinate. My accented English and my bookish appearance may have created that impression. However, in later years, when Dr. Finkelstein fell ill, I became the pulpit rabbi of an impromptu congregation, consisting mostly of young people, which at first met in Dr. Finkelstein's apartment and then was relocated to a Jewish home for the aged, where it continues to this day. This experience makes me suspect that had I entered the pulpit rabbinate I would have made a success of it.

It seems that even after my meeting with Dr. Finkelstein, the committee still was not completely sure of me, for when I decided to go to Ramah, a summer camp under the auspices of the Seminary, the faculty asked the professor-in-residence, a teacher who was the Seminary representative in camp, to keep an eye on me and report back to the faculty at its first meeting of the school year on whether my goal was really scholarship.

The professor-in-residence then was Dr. Gerson D. Cohen, who later succeeded Dr. Finkelstein as chancellor of the Seminary, and with whom I enjoyed a lengthy friendship until a severe falling out took place between us over the scholarly and religious policy of the Seminary. Dr.

Cohen's report was positive, very positive. ("You passed with flying colors," I was told by a faculty member who was present at the meeting when the report was made.) This was further confirmed a year later, when I was asked to come back to Camp Ramah and to prepare a few bright students to enter the Seminary. Among them was the present chancellor of the Seminary, Dr. Ismar Schorsch, who, forty years later, wrote: "In 1955 . . . I came to the Poconos to study Talmud in a special study group and to be transformed forever." Thus begun my association with Camp Ramah, which lasted almost twenty-five years—I served as professor-in-residence in various Ramah camps —during which I endeavored to retain the old religious policy of the Seminary, though not without occasional deviations to pacify the contending factions. As long as these deviations did not harden into principles, but remained clearly local and provisional compromises, and as long as they did not violate basic religous behavior, I was more susceptible to modern sensibilities.

In late September of 1954, Dr. Finkelstein called me and said: "Here is a $4,000 fellowship (tax-free). From now on, let me have your *daiges parnasa*—let me worry about your livelihood. You sit and learn." It is difficult to imagine what that meant to me. It was the first time in my life that I had an income and did not have to worry about how I would support myself. Hunger was familiar to me. In my grandfather's home, even before we were taken to the ghetto, I hardly ate enough and was always on the verge of being undernourished. In America, I had enough to eat but it was always a hand-to-mouth existence. Especially when I married, and planned to have a family, the financial uncertainty weighed heavily upon me.

I was never sure what would be available the next day. To have a steady income without worry about tomorrow, to have health insurance without worry about what would happen if we became sick, and to be able to devote all my time to study was paradise. I was grateful to Dr. Finkelstein for that gesture. Years later, when he was sick and old (he died in his ninety-sixth year), on one of my frequent visits to him I found him crying, expressing doubts about his life's work in light of the changes that had recently taken place in the Seminary. I told him, "Dr. Finkelstein, if you had done nothing else but what you did for me, a lost soul of the Holocaust, your place would be secure."

LEAVING THE Seminary in 1985 after more than thirty years of association was very painful. It took me some time until I could bring myself to visit it again. I had peaceful years in the Seminary, free from interference, friendly, and devoted almost exclusively to study. I attracted students and with many of them formed lasting relationships that have not diminished to this day. I taught a minimum course load, and I taught what I wanted to teach, which more often than not was a try-out of what I was doing creatively. My theory about the composition of the Talmud was hatched and developed during that period. In my mind I spun various theological constructs, mistakenly believing them to be suitable for the Conservative movement, and I relished being one of its leaders.

The Seminary at that time was heavily paternalistic, but being the recipient of its benefits, its fair-haired boy, I was not much aware of it. The scholarly atmosphere was dominated by the high standard set by Professor Lieberman, attracting visitors, teachers, and the great Jewish scholars of the time. To a young scholar aspiring to make his own mark on scholarship—equal to theirs but different—it was just what the doctor ordered. There was no better training school. Even when I deviated (and I did deviate in method and outlook, which for a while gave rise to friction), I did so on the strength of what I learned then and there. I was happy at the Seminary and entertained no desire to leave. After all I had been through, I had finally found respite.

All this changed with the new administration—the one that succeeded Dr. Finkelstein—headed by Dr. Gerson Cohen. The beginning seemed to herald harmonious cooperation between us, with him in an administrative role and me in an academic one. Jointly, we would rejuvenate the Seminary. I had every reason to believe that this harmony would continue, for we were friends of long standing. Years before, in 1958, I had received my doctorate from the Seminary on the basis of my edition of a fourteenth-century manuscript. It was Dr. Cohen, who then served as librarian of the splendid Jewish Theological Seminary Library, who called my attention to this manuscript, and I acknowledged my indebtedness to him in the preface of the printed edition. We often saw each other and held many scholarly discussions. Dr. Cohen would consult me on textual matters and I him on historical events. He spoke favorably of me to others, and I reciprocated, publicly supporting his candidacy for the position of chancellor. Some saw in him and me successors to Dr. Finkelstein and Dr. Lieberman respectively.

Soon, however, Dr. Cohen embarked on reforms (the

ordination of women was the most conspicuous but not the only one) which I believed negated halakhah, Jewish law. At first, out of loyalty to him, I searched for precedents, trying to find in the rich Rabbinic literature opinions in favor of the reforms. I would have gone along if those opinions had been held by a small minority, even if rejected by the overwhelming majority. Considering the women's issue today as a kind of *sh'at hadehak*, an emergency situation, I would have followed the Talmud and relied on a minority view, which can also be reflected in a new reading of a text. I made some suggestions (among them, that women take upon themselves the observance of *time-bound commandments* from which, traditionally, they were exempted) which would symbolize submission to halakhah, to the divine writ, and hence to God, and which might have reflected precedents. I even wrote a responsum outlining this view, which I later withdrew. My proposal was rejected as insufficiently egalitarian, because it maintained some restrictions on women and because its effect would not have been felt until a new generation of women grew up whose mothers observed the time-bound commandments, thus obligating their daughters halakhically to do the same, as an expression of *Torat imecha*, "the instruction of your mother" (Proverbs 1:8). But without antecedent support, I would not tamper with any law or custom.

I began to feel uncomfortable at the Seminary, but I still stayed, partly out of inertia and partly out of my perennial fear that if I left I would have to look for another position, which I might not find. There were also academic changes that I did not approve of. Talmud and rabbinics were always the chief subjects in any seminary's curricu-

lum. They were supposed to be the most closely related to
the activities of a rabbi, what a rabbi must know to conduct the religious affairs of his congregation. These subjects might be taught at the Seminary in a different manner
from that in the yeshivot, but both institutions attributed
supreme importance to them. The new administration
changed the traditional curricular focus of the Seminary
from Talmud and rabbinics to history. The rationale behind this change (besides the fact that the chancellor was
a historian who was more comfortable with history than
with Talmud and rabbinics) was probably that the modern Conservative rabbi is asked few halakhic questions,
and an intelligent knowledge of Jewish history would be
of greater use to him—a rationale that gives in to a de
facto situation instead of trying to change that situation.

My chasidic upbringing had accustomed me to the fact
that it is usually the right that is oppressive; the more *frum*
one is—the more believing and observant one is—the
more liable one is to force others to believe and behave
like oneself. The less religious tend to be more tolerant.
Now, however, carrying out the reforms became a religious commitment, and those who disagreed or spoke to
the contrary were unceremoniously silenced. As the debate
heated up, the atmosphere became more oppressive.

Once at a faculty meeting I prepared a rebuttal, and
when I rose to speak the chancellor ordered me to sit
down. That elicited a protest from Rabbi Joel Roth (one
of the younger faculty members, who later became the
architect of the responsum supporting women's ordination), who remonstrated, "Will you let our teacher
speak?" The chancellor was dismayed at Rabbi Roth's te-
merity, but he did let me speak.

Just a few years before, it had been decided that the Seminary's Friday night service, which had a poor attendance, should include a *d'var Torah*, a ten-minute "sermonette." Within a year or two, Friday night services at the Seminary were drawing as many as two hundred young people. I usually gave the sermonette, and after 1979, when the ordination of women became quite a divisive issue, the chancellor periodically monitored my speeches. Once I spoke on Friday night about the famous story of Rabbi Joshua, the first-century scholar of the land of Israel who, having calculated the calendar differently from his colleagues, nonetheless submitted to Raban Gamaliel's prompting and went out with his staff and money on the day which, by his own reckoning, was Yom Kippur, the Day of Atonement. I added that this kind of obedience, against one's own judgment, applies only in matters of calendar reckoning, in order not to split the community into different sects, each one celebrating the holidays on different dates; but it does not otherwise apply when one is directed, even by a man of the stature of Raban Gamaliel (who was the *Nasi*, the Patriarch), to do something against one's religious conscience. In matters other than the calendar, the religious conscience must always prevail.

On Sunday morning I received a call from the chancellor chiding me for agitating against the decision in favor of the reforms. When I asked him, "Do you want me to discontinue my *divrei Torah*?" he said, "No, not yet, for you would then become a martyr."

Tensions mounted and spilled into personal relationships, forcing us into even more inflexible stances. When Professor Lieberman died in 1983, Dr. Cohen did not ask me to deliver the eulogy even though I was then the chairman of the Talmud and Rabbinics Department. He also notified me that he was about to circulate a letter to the faculty saying that, starting with the next Sabbath, I would no longer be the rabbi of the Seminary's synagogue—a position that I had held whenever Professor Lieberman was away. When I subsequently asked him, "What are you signaling, Gerson?" he told me, "I want to break the Lieberman syndrome." I took that to mean that, besides dethroning Talmud, which at the Seminary was associated with Lieberman's name, he also wanted to get the Seminary and its faculty more involved in the community life of the average Conservative congregation (prior to that, the Seminary was primarily an academic institution) and that I stood in his way.

This attitude on the part of Dr. Cohen was rather surprising, for up to a short time before the vote on the reforms, he advocated a strict separation between personal relationships of long standing and disagreements of recent vintage concerning Seminary policy. Perhaps he saw in my sermonettes a violation of this separation, an attempt to sow disunity, to incite students to become conscientious objectors to his reforms, which he apparently took as a personal affront. That was far from my intention. My intention was to defend myself against the citing of the Raban Gamaliel and Rabbi Joshua story as a paradigm of the academy submitting to the administration. I had reason to believe that Dr. Cohen intended to use this story of Raban Gamaliel and Rabbi Joshua to calm the consciences of those few faculty members who still had unresolved scruples about voting for the reforms, to tell them that no matter how fierce a debate may be, ultimately the leader's point of view must prevail, at least in the public domain. By stating categorically that the story applies uniquely to issues of the calendar I removed a weapon from his polemical arsenal. This move may have provoked the unusual counterreaction of my being sidelined whenever possible in order to impede my influence. My not being asked to deliver the eulogy for Professor Lieberman was one example of this policy.

The chancellor overestimated my influence. Having decided to carry out the reforms and fearing a backlash, he brooked no resistance, real or imagined. But there was no need for that attitude. With the overwhelming majority of the Conservative movement behind him (which he may not have known), he could have achieved his goal with gentler tactics.

WHAT FINALLY convinced me that I had to leave the Seminary was not so much the actual decision in favor of the reforms. On the contrary, I greatly sympathize with some of the problems they addressed and am trying to alleviate them by recruiting serious female students to the Talmud program at Columbia University, with the hope that when they become scholars they themselves will discover solutions. Rather, the implications of the process and decision were intolerable to me. The reforms were interpreted to mean that halakhah had bowed to modernity. A single infraction of a law, even of the magnitude of these reforms, can be isolated, can be cordoned off and distanced with little or no impact on the other laws or on the system as a whole. That probably would have happened had a similar infraction taken place in a small

Jewish community, free of the influence of Reform or *Haskalah* (Enlightenment). But in the present climate of opinion, doing away with a law which the media and the modern temper have little sympathy for (and may even consider immoral) will, *ipso facto*, be interpreted as a clash between modernity and halakhah in general, with the latter retreating. Halakhah is then reduced to the status of folklore or at best to a mode of behavior that served Jews well in the past but, like everything else in history, needs periodic adjustments to be viable today. That will set a pattern for the future: whenever halakhah and modernity collide, halakhah yields. A halakhah that yields to anybody or anything cannot be Divine in the traditional sense of being revealed, which, in the words of Leo Strauss, is "the central idea of the Bible and the condition of the possibility of all the others." This shakes the very foundation on which Jewish belief was based throughout the ages and inevitably weakens adherence to its precepts.

Realizing the detrimental nature of these implications, some of which I believe has been confirmed since then, I felt a need not only to disassociate myself from the decision by voting against it but also to reassert the supremacy of the halakhah as the sole vehicle for a Jew's getting close to God. I expressed my sentiments in the following letter, which I sent to the faculty members at the time they voted on the reforms (the first sentence of the last paragraph I heard from the late Professor Ernest Simon):

To the members of the Faculty Assembly:
My position concerning women's ordination is by now, I take it, well known to all of you assembled here.

I am against it. It is a violation of *halakhah* which to me is sufficient grounds to reject it.

I am cognizant of the enormous pressure exerted upon us from different quarters to ordain women. But a religious Jew, when faced with a confrontation between sociology and religion, must choose religion. This is the meaning of *kabbalat 'ol mitzvot*, of accepting the yoke of the mitzvot; even if it is uncomfortable, even if it is being attacked and ridiculed, and even if you have doubts about its ethical correctness. As in the case of its counterpart, *kabbalat 'ol malkhut shamayim*, the acceptance of the yoke of the kingdom of heaven, one does not abandon faith in God every time one has a doubt—every time one has a question. Doubts pass and a stronger faith emerges in their wake. True love is tormented love; after making up, the soul is at greater peace than before the quarrel. It is easy to have faith when one is sure of God's existence, secure in the knowledge that He is caring for him. The task is to reach out to heaven when it is cloudy, when no heaven is visible. Truly religious Jews came out of concentration camps strengthened in their faith, fortified in their commitment to Judaism. They could not afford losing everything. "Though he may slay me, yet in him I will trust" (Job 13:15).

I have studied, restudied and examined the examples some scholars say indicate that the Rabbis *consciously* changed a law for either ethical or moral reasons. I have found *no* tangible evidence to support such a thesis. Indeed, I would have been very much surprised were it different. For that would have impugned the ethical or moral integrity of their predecessors. It would have implied that they imagined themselves to be superior to their teachers and to their teachers' teachers, up to the first link in the chain of tradition. Such a thought, if ever it occurred to them, would have been immediately banished and suppressed. It runs counter to their notion of the sanctity of tradition, which in order to be grounded in revelation—the ultimate religious authority—had to assume that the closer one gets to the time and source of revelation, the more reliable and authoritative is his teaching.

That is not to say that there were no changes in halakhah, that halakhah remained monolithic throughout the ages. Changes did take place, *but they were not done consciously.* The scholars who legalized them did not perceive themselves as innovators. The changes were integrated into community life long before they sought—and received—legal sanction. They originally came about imperceptibly, unnoticed, the result of a gradual evolutionary process. By the time they demanded legal justification, they were ripe, overgrown, as it were. So much so, that in many an instance, whoever opposed the changes was considered a breaker of tradition, adopting a "holier than thou" attitude.

A Jew knows no other way of reaching out to God other than through halakhah (the latter taken in the widest possible sense). He knows no way to penetrate the highest recesses of spirituality other than through a structured pattern of behavior. In the course of that engagement he may experience a sense of elevation, a touch of ecstasy, a feeling of being near to God. That is his greatest reward. While it lasts, he is desirous of nothing more. Indeed, nothing else exists.

How does a *mitzvah* catapult one into such religious heights? What is prayer? Nobody knows, any more than we know when looking at the sunset, or at a smiling child, how and why we are gripped, riveted to the scene, transformed in a foretaste of the world to come. Our religious and aesthetic experiences are shrouded in mystery. We are put on fire, but do not know how the fire is being kindled. The mistake of reform is that it claims that it knows how the fire is being kindled; that, as a result, it can control the flame. When it actually tried to control the flame, alas there was no fire; everything was so cold!

The truly religious Jew is awe-stricken both by the mystery of God and by the efficacy of the mitzvot to bring man closer to God. He dares not tamper with the mitzvot for he humbly acknowledges that he knows not their secret, or secrets. He is grateful to the tradition for having kept alive through the ages the connection between God and the performance of the mitzvot, so that he can now relive it, re-experience it and bequeath it to his children. Without tradition, he would not have found his way to God; it is his religious lifeline. He cannot part from it.

In the light of the above, I hope you will understand why I cannot participate in the vote on women's ordination scheduled for October 24, 1983. I am committed to Jewish tradition in all of its various aspects. I cannot, therefore, participate in a debate on a religious issue of major historical significance where the traditional decision-making process is not sufficiently

honored; its specific instructions as to who is qualified
to pass judgment not sufficiently reckoned with. Even
to strengthen tradition, one must proceed traditionally.
Otherwise it is a *mitzvah haba'ah ba'aveirah*—a mitzvah performed by means of a transgression.

It is my personal tragedy that the people I *daven*
[pray] with, I cannot talk to, and the people I talk to,
I cannot *daven* with. However, when the chips are
down, I will always side with the people I *daven* with;
for I can live without talking. I cannot live without
davening.

David Halivni

Now, when I look back on this emotionally charged
letter—composed hours before the vote took place—I realize that I might stand accused of inconsistency, of will-
ingness to follow reason against tradition in pursuing
critical study, but unwillingness to follow morality against
tradition, rejecting changes alleged to be motivated by ethical considerations. Why compromise with tradition intellectually but not behaviorally? My only defense is that I
have greater confidence in our sense of reason than in
what we consider moral. I consider the former more objective and am therefore less willing to compromise on it,
a distinction that not everyone is willing to make, certainly
not to honor. The awareness of this lack of universal approval does not not necessarily vitiate my conviction; it
does, however, diminish the vehemence of my argument,
allowing for greater understanding of the opposing position.

AFTER THE vote I felt the need for a change of atmosphere. I decided to take advantage of a sabbatical that was coming to me, and went to Israel, seriously considering settling there. Apparently, others thought I might remain there as well, for the city of Tel Aviv awarded me the Bialik Prize (Israel's equivalent of the Pulitzer), which, with rare exceptions, is generally given only to Israelis. I entertained offers of teaching positions in Israel. In the meantime, however, I received a communication from the dean of the Graduate School at Columbia University (with which I had been associated as an adjunct professor since 1961) telling me not to make any commitments, for something might work out; and indeed it did. A year and a half later I was back in New York and teaching at Columbia. The initial apprehension of some members of the administration at Columbia about whether there would be students interested in Talmud and rabbinics proved entirely unwarranted. There are more students than I can handle, even with an assistant. My personal apprehension about whether or not I would be happy in a non-Jewish environment (some of my colleagues at the Seminary predicted that I would not be) proved equally unwarranted. I find the atmosphere at Columbia congenial, have acquired new friends inside and outside the department, and despite occasional annoyances enjoy my stay at the university. It is agreeable and stimulating to my creative endeavors.

5

AFTERMATH

My Life Now

WHEN I look back at my experiences in the ghetto and in the concentration camp I do not remember ever having felt that the end was near, that my life would soon be extinguished. At no point was I seized with mortal fear that I might not make it, that my death was imminent. Somehow, I was confident that I still had life ahead of me and would survive. Anti-Semitism was a part of my very being. I have suffered under it for as long as I remember; it dates back to the dawn of my self-awareness. But it was not life-threatening until the harsh period between the German occupation of Hungary, on March 19, 1944, and my liberation by the Americans in Ebensee-Mauthausen, Upper Austria, on May 6, 1945, during which period actual killing was the order of the day. Yet even during this time, I was confident of my survival.

MY FIRST camp after Auschwitz, Gross-Rosen, in Lower Silesia, could be classified as a "moderate" camp. People were not killed there for the sake of killing. However, many died needlessly there as well. The first Sigheter to die there was Laibl Kahan, the son of Nachum Hersh Kahan, the gabai, the right hand of the Chief Rabbi of Sighet. A tree fell on him. There were other such "accidents" that could have been avoided. But the aim of the camp was not to impose death on the inmates, to exterminate them. That changed when I came to Ebensee, where they killed just for the sake of killing. Hundreds of fresh deportees arrived daily, but the number of inmates remained the same or even decreased. Ebensee was one of the worst camps—it was an avowed extermination camp. It lasted until May 6, 1945, six days after Hitler committed suicide. A few days before liberation, we were ordered to gather at the *Appellplatz*—the place where the prisoners were counted—and the multitude there shouted in unison, "No, no!" I did not know it at the time, but I read subsequently in a book on the history of Mauthausen that the shouting was in defiance of the *Lagerkommandant*'s attempt to herd us into the nearby tunnel and kill us there with explosives. The people dared to resist. The kapos knew of the sinister plan and organized collective resistance. They prevailed because the guards knew that the war was lost and refused to obey. The event is chronicled as "the only revolt known in the history of Mauthausen."

Even at Ebensee, as far as I can recollect, I did not give up on life. The evidence around me attested to the contrary: that nobody would survive, that death would claim all of us. Yet I refused to succumb to the evidence and, despite it, was confident that I would not die in the camp and that a future was still awaiting me.

In fact, I remember that in Ebensee I once met Oskar (Ossie) Dob and his father (whose first name escapes me, but I remember that he and his brother were cattle dealers). The Dobs were neighbors of ours in Sighet, and Ossie's mother was very friendly with my mother. Every time Mother went to visit the family, she would come back and give me an argument because "Ossie looks healthy and athletic," and I was pale and thin from sitting all day long in the synagogue, where the walls were damp and the windows were stuck shut with paint.

In Ebensee I came across the Dobs when the son was showing recognizable signs of imminent death. We called people who were about to die of starvation *muselmänner*. The father was standing over his son, crying and ranting and pleading with me to remember them to their relatives: "You, Dovid, you will survive. Go home and tell my cousin"—he had a cousin we all called (I do not know why) Cigan Primash, who lived on the Romanian side of the border where Jews were not deported and who therefore was assumed to be alive. The father grabbed me and sobbed, "Tell him of our suffering here, what Ossie and I are going through." A few hours later, Ossie died.

ANOTHER TIME when I was told that I would survive was in Ungvár in 1942. While there, I met a Jew by the name of Joshua Heschel Friedmann, and slept in his house. He told me, "I will not survive the war. I am too old. You will. I want to be remembered. Here is a *shtikel*

Torah [a piece of Torah, a new interpretation of a biblical passage]. Repeat it in my name after I am gone."

Mr. Friedmann's *shtikel* Torah is in the spirit of pilpul, which may not be appreciated by those who were not brought up on it. Yet the beauty of stringing together separate passages to form an integrated whole should impress everyone who takes the trouble to read it carefully.

The text in question is the dialogue between Joseph and Judah in Genesis 44, and it concerns specifically verse 10. Judah has suggested (in verse 9) that whichever of his brothers stole the silver goblet from Joseph's table "shall die, and the rest of us shall become slaves." To this, Joseph (or, rather, his steward, quoting him) retorts, "Now, too, let it be according to your words: he with whom the silver goblet shall be found shall be a slave, and you shall go free." The commentators are puzzled by the expression, "Now, too," which suggests that this is the second time that Judah, or his brothers, make such a suggestion, while we have no record that such was the case.

To explicate this passage, Mr. Friedmann utilized a well-known Rabbinic interpretation concerning the sale into captivity of Joseph by his brothers. According to the Bible, the brothers sold Joseph because they were jealous of the preferential treatment he received from their father. The Rabbis of the Talmud found this explanation too degrading of the brothers' moral stature. Instead, they posited that Joseph and his brothers were engaged in a fierce Talmudic debate and that, according to the brothers' view, Joseph had committed a serious infraction for which he deserved such punishment. One late-medieval scholar suggested, as a possible topic of this debate, the question of whether, even though they lived before God gave the

Torah to Moses on Sinai, Joseph and his brothers were nevertheless bound by the Mosaic code, which they knew by means of prophecy. If they were not so bound, one side of this debate would reason, then, like everybody else, they would be subject to the contemporary local laws, which, according to the account of the medieval commentator, were generally more severe. Joseph was of the opinion that his family was bound to follow the more strict local code (and held his brothers to this standard), whereas the brothers believed that they were bound only by the more lenient Mosaic code.

Several examples of the legal discrepancy are given in the traditional sources. The most bizarre one claims that Joseph saw his brothers ritually slaughtering an animal and eating a fetus found in its womb. According to Rabbinic law a fetus is part of its mother, and it becomes fit for eating through the kosher slaughtering of its mother, whereas according to the supposed local custom the dead fetus is considered an independent animal that has died a natural death and whose meat is therefore forbidden as food. Joseph was of this latter opinion, while his brothers followed the more lenient Rabbinic code.

Let me add that while this example may seem bizarre to us, it was not so to the ancients. The recently published Dead Sea Scroll known as M.M.T. reflects a dispute on this very matter among the various sectarians.

Mr. Friedmann's contribution was the suggestion that, ultimately, the brothers and Joseph traded positions on this issue. Beset by their own troubles in Egypt, the brothers, imagining Joseph's hardship, said to one another, "Alas, we are being punished on account of our brother, because we looked on at his anguish, yet paid no heed as he pleaded with us" (Genesis 42:21). The brothers came to the conclusion that they were wrong to punish Joseph, that he had indeed been right to require their adherence to the strict local laws. Joseph, on the other hand, having suffered at the hand of Potiphar and in the prison, came to the opposite conclusion: that he had been wrong, and his brothers right to require adherence to the Mosaic law alone. When it came to punishing the one who, apparently, had stolen the silver goblet, both Joseph and his brothers expressed their new positions: Judah representing the more strict position, and Joseph the more lenient. Judah suggested that the thief be put to death, and the remaining brothers enslaved (apparently, the strict local custom); whereas Joseph followed the Mosaic law, which dictates that only the thief himself is culpable, and does not demand that he suffer the death penalty. Joseph prefaced his statement with the words "Now, too, let it be according to your words," that is, your earlier words, and your former position, in our father's house, that we ought to conduct our affairs according to the Mosaic law, which punishes only the thief, with bondage, and not to a foreign, harsher code.

Mr. Friedmann died during the war, and he left me with his "mission." That mission weighed heavily on me. His grandson had been with me in the Gross-Rosen camp, and I had wanted to give him the piece of Torah to relieve me of the responsibility of remembering. But he did not survive. So every year since the war when the Torah portion of the week included the passage of the Bible that Mr. Friedmann interpreted, I used to repeat the piece of Torah in public, in his name, until my own children knew it by heart. Finally I insisted that his other son, who had come to New York before the war with Mr. Friedmann's grandson, record the piece of Torah. After he did so, I felt liberated.

THAT I survived was no surprise to me. I took it for granted. I had a built-in belief that God would grant me life and would not abandon me there. There were so many things to do, so many things to learn, so many songs to sing that I was certain God would grant me the privilege of partaking of some of them.

However, I did not escape unscathed. I am living in the aftermath. When I examine my life now, I believe I can discern traces of the fear and anguish that I must have imbibed during this horrible period. I was not able to perceive them before. Patterns of behavior that grip me now can best be explained as subconscious outbursts that originated then and now periodically come to the fore to plague me: a wound that is not wholly healed, a memory that refuses to go away. Both my physical and my spiritual life are affected, separately and jointly. While after the war I had nightmares—who didn't?—they gradually disappeared, though not entirely. Occasionally they would come back, but basically they were no hindrance to my sleep. The fears in the nightmares, or "daymares," however, seem to have been internalized, suppressed in the subconscious, and they manifested themselves in other ways.

For instance, I feel a constant anxiety, which I attribute to a fear of death. I was once in a car with a famous psychiatrist. After he came in, I locked the door, innocently, without even being aware of having done so. The doctor nonchalantly asked me, "Are you afraid of death?" The fear manifests itself when I visit doctors. As soon as I go to a doctor, my systolic blood pressure rises beyond its normal rate. My doctor knows already that I have to wait and have it measured again, that I need reassurance before it goes down. I have difficulty when I go to any other doctor for other things. A doctor automatically takes one's blood pressure, and I have to tell any doctor ahead of time, "You had better measure it more than once." I once went to a dentist to have a tooth extracted. He wanted to take my blood pressure, and I told him that he would have to take it several times. He refused to do that. I called my doctor, who told him over the phone to gave me a little Valium, and within a few minutes my blood pressure went back to normal. Many years ago a doctor who did not know of my special nervous condition gave me a medicine against high blood pressure. That scared me into thinking that I really had high blood pressure, and I fell into a kind of anxiety, a panic attack that took me almost a year to get out of. During that time I tried to fight it with the only power at my disposal, with learning.

I even remember what I learned. It was the Babylonian Talmud, Tractate *Yoma* 52b. I learned it more or less the traditional way, the way I had studied in Sighet, the way most traditional institutions study it today, not critically, the way I now study it. For critical study you first learn the text according to the traditional interpretations, with the commentaries that have accumulated on the Talmud for the last sixteen or seventeen hundred years, and then you look at these commentaries and interpretations and ask: Do they honor the integrity of the text, the context, the tenor of the words? Do the words support the interpretation, or is the interpretation forced upon the words? Do you have to shrink some of the text? Would the text be better if certain of its words were not there? You also ask, conversely: Do you have to add something to the text? Are the words as presently constituted insufficient to contain the attributed interpretation? If the answer is yes, the interpretation is considered forced, and according to the critical method, something must have gone wrong in the transmission of the text that gave rise to the forced interpretation. To overcome that, one has to go back in time, trace the steps of the transmission, point out where the transmission went wrong, and reassemble the pieces in a manner that will obviate the forced interpretation. This kind of process is rather difficult. Some people never take to it, for it requires the dismantling and reassembling of the text.

Standard Talmud scholarship assumes "contiguity of knowledge"—that the late sages had an absolute knowledge of the statements of the early sages, knew their contents and the circumstances that gave rise to them. And when there are blemishes—forced interpretations or implausible assertions—they must be overcome either through a better reading of the text or through a better explanation.

We critical scholars do not share this assumption. We do not suppose "contiguity of knowledge" as an absolute given. And when there are blemishes, we suspect a defect in transmission—that the statements did not reach the later sages adequately and completely. The blemishes are not overcome; at best we can explain how they came into being, how the historical process gave rise to them. They are not removed. To some people the existence of blemishes is inconsistent with the religious stature of the Talmud. A revelatory document in any form should be free of such defects. And they shun a method that posits such limitations.

At the time that I felt this anxiety, I learned traditionally. I didn't introduce critical thinking, which had been my mode of study for more than fifteen years. Then I attributed the deviation to the difficulty of critical learning when one is in a state of anxiety. In that state, one chooses the easier method. It's difficult to study complicated subjects when one is stressed and not in the mood to learn altogether. Now I see the deviation more as reverting to my background in Sighet, where studying with Grandfather was my guarantee, my assurance of security. All the difficulties I experienced at home were compensated for by my learning, by the respect I got for it at home and from the community; when I felt threatened again, I reverted to the traditional study I did in my earlier years, the kind that gave me security.

SOME YEARS ago there was an article in *The New York Times Magazine* about me. The writer, Israel Shenker, ended the article with one of the many stories I had told him: During the student revolt in 1968, I was once walking along 116th Street near Riverside Drive, toward Broadway, in the vicinity of Columbia University, where I was an adjunct professor and teaching Judaica. I met students who were protesting, demanding "relevance," and when they noticed me they stared at me with disdain—or so I thought. I was the epitome of non-relevance. I offered them religious texts of two thousand years ago, philological and historical study, with minimal emphasis on social and political events. When they looked at me they saw a relic, an antiquarian, and had little interest in me or in what I taught. Since I always craved approval, I was very much affected by their attitude.

Shenker asked me, "So what did you do?" and I said, "I did what I always do when I feel upset. I went back, to 116th Street and Riverside, to my home; I went upstairs, took out a Talmud, and learned. Except this time, my eyes were wet. I had tears in my eyes, and I couldn't very well see what I was learning." To this day, when I feel downcast for no discernible reason, I will take out a Talmud and study. After I score a *chiddush*, an innovation, after I have discovered some new twist, I will regain my composure.

PERHAPS MORE than most people, at the slightest symptom I am likely to be struck by fear of having contracted a serious life-threatening disease. A slight cough, for instance, will easily trigger a fear that I have pneumonia, TB, or even lung cancer, which in turn will release anxiety pangs that dull creative pleasures and require a redoubling of energy to overcome irritability and to go on with everyday life.

I never cease to be amazed at how close to the surface the threshold of anxiety is. At the slightest provocation, and apparently under any condition, it appears gnawing under the heart as if it were there all along, just waiting for an opportune moment to strike.

Since I do not remember having suffered from the fear

of death in Sighet, I attribute this malaise to my experience in the ghetto and the camps. I imbibed it there, internalized it, and felt the effects after liberation.

ANOTHER ASPECT of my internalization could be that, for fifty years afterward, I did not speak about the Holocaust. I used to say semi-jokingly in reference to my friend and fellow Sigheter Elie Wiesel, "He speaks and I am quiet"—although we more or less went on a similar journey—"but when we meet, I shout and he listens."

So I didn't speak. And even when my children begged me to tell them of my experience, I would give them minimal, dry facts and never detail them. I certainly didn't enjoy talking about it; I ran away from reliving that particular age.

On the other hand, I followed every bit of literature on the *Shoah* I could lay my hands on; every event that was connected with it had meaning to me. I read about it with relish. I felt an affinity with every person who was associated with the Shoah. When there was an evaluation or comparison of it, I was alert. Most of the time I advocated the uniqueness of the Holocaust, without necessarily minimizing any of the other catastrophes in human history.

When I married, in 1953, I did not speak of the Shoah at the wedding, though I was well aware of the belief that the souls of departed parents join their children under the wedding canopy; but I did do so when my youngest son, Shai, married Diane Kushnir forty years later. Nevertheless, in public, I did not speak or lecture about the Holocaust, although I listened to lectures about it. I stayed away from the subject until fifty years later, when by co-incidence I was asked to deliver a lecture on the fiftieth anniversary of the liberation of Hungarian Jewry. I was staying in Israel at the time, and when I got a call in the early morning hours, I thought I said, "I don't do that." I was sure I had said no, but afterward I was told that I had agreed, that I did not decline as usual, that I was already billed, already on the program. This began my interest in talking about the Holocaust—my journey out of silence, out of the closet, as it were—and preparing this memoir.

I think the reason for my silence was not only that I did not want to relive the pain of telling the story but much more basic, more essential. Speaking of my experiences challenged my sense of security. Deep down in my subconscious, the injury has not yet healed, the wound has not closed, the trauma has not left. In those deep recesses, there is still a fear that it may all come back, that my life is still in danger, and talking about it will intensify its reappearance. Not talking is a sort of covering up, of banishing it so that it will go away, or at least stay where it is and not come to the surface.

A THIRD aspect of the aftermath, besides the anxiety and not wanting to talk about the Holocaust, is that when I look at my intimate friends I find few Holocaust survivors. Being a Holocaust survivor is ingrained in my flesh—and even my tombstone will say that I was a survivor. A few months ago I was very much taken with a writer's suggestion that Holocaust survivors should have a special mark put on their tombstones for identification. I don't like the idea of a mark, but I plan to have engraved on the tombstone that I am one of the *nitzolei haShoah*, a survivor of the Holocaust. I think of a similar act by the Jews who were expelled from Spain in 1492: in whatever they wrote, those who were expelled and those who came after them mentioned that they were survivors or descendants of survivors of the expulsion.

Nevertheless, my friends are not those who survived, although I follow and crave reading about the survivors and their activity. They are of deep concern to me, but they don't constitute my circle of intimate friends. I married a survivor, my wife Tzipora is one, but she is part of myself. Outside, however, I am not close to them. I recognize in many an attitude that indicates they are still reliving the trauma. I believe that Art Spiegelman, who wrote *Maus*, mentions that his father, a survivor, used to play with the gas range in his bungalow, lighting cigarettes from a burner. The children would be annoyed because gas is not made to light cigarettes, to use instead of a match; gas is made to cook and bake. But they discovered later that to their father gas meant something else, and he was reliving the experience by playing with it off and on, which was really playing off and on with his life, with his fears.

Normally, people like us who suffered so much starvation find it easy to fast one day a year, and a fast day should pass by without too much attention or difficulty. However, I know a survivor who at ten o'clock on Yom Kippur morning (a religious fast day) is already sweating, whose face is bloated, who is visibly suffering from pangs of hunger. In his subconscious he is transported to camp life fifty years earlier, sees himself there, and is afraid that this is a hunger that will last forever, that will ultimately kill him. He is tormented by subconscious fear.

These traits call for sympathy, affinity, and understanding, and I empathize with several Holocaust survivors I have met with similar traits. But they are not my close friends. After the war I once read that many survivors did not want to be treated by doctors who themselves were survivors. Except for Elie Wiesel—who is a higher and different spiritual being—my friends are not survivors. Could it be because survivors are living reminders of the past and seeing them is reliving the past? Somewhere, deep down, the experience has been encased and concealed, has not been totally eradicated, has not been forgotten, has not been overcome. It is still there, locked in the subconscious. On occasion it opens and threatens me.

THERE IS a streak of meekness in me. I am always on the defensive, eager to please and ready to give in. Students sometimes take advantage of this streak and bargain for a higher grade when it is not due them or say things that are outrageously wrong, knowing that I will not criticize them to their faces. I have difficulty criticizing people to their faces. I will be reassuring even when it is not warranted. If I do not like what I hear, I will either beat around the bush if confronted, or remain silent if I am a mere listener. I will not taunt or insult.

Such an attitude is generally considered religiously laudable. But to a religious person it does not come easily. It comes after a battle with antagonistic inclinations, after a conquest of contrary desires. In my case, however, it seems to have been imprinted on me without an inner fight, something that I sought out as a mode of self-defense. I therefore attribute it to my having been dependent as a child on the goodwill of the community to counterbalance the adversity I experienced at home. The meekness is the result of my craving for approval, the achievement of which served me well in weathering the many hardships that were my share when I was young. Arguing or criticizing somebody makes for a contentious atmosphere, a confrontation I do not bear easily.

I am also given to panic. When confronting an unexpected threatening situation, instead of soberly reviewing the possible options available to avoid the threat I will be seized by a fear that paralyzes rational action. If I am locked in a room, I will pound wildly on the door rather than apply the key more intelligently. More than the people around me, I fear unlikely accidents, worry about them, rationalize them. When I lecture or speak without notes, which I prefer, I might be seized with the fear that I will forget the appropriate quotation.

I remember times when I was called upon in the synagogue to recite the blessings before reading the Torah—words that I have known since I remember myself and whose content I have studied and written about—and I was fearful that I might not remember the blessings. My good memory also did not always shield me from panicking in a test that required the use of mathematical formulas. Once, during a math exam, I was afraid that I did not correctly remember a formula, and I tried to derive it anew, which delayed my completion of the test and affected my grade.

More significant for this memoir is that I have a reputation of having an excellent memory. People exaggerate when they say I have a photographic memory: in the course of the years I have developed my above-average memory into a useful instrument to retain textual materials. Be that as it may, it is startling that I have almost no recollection of the days I spent in Auschwitz. I remember vividly my arrival there, the ramp, the rooms where we were shaved and where we changed into prison clothes, but nothing beyond that. Of my stay in Auschwitz proper, I have "blacked out" all but a discussion with a Sigheter by the name of Chaim Lieberman, who tried to convince me of something I was already convinced of: that if I wanted to survive I had to eat non-kosher food—as if even non-kosher food were sufficiently available in Auschwitz. I remember leaving Auschwitz, the layout of the car in the train that took us out of Auschwitz, who sat where, the names of the Sigheters who were there, the threatening posture of the SS man who accompanied and sat with us in the car, but not what happened before our leaving, nothing between the arrival and the departure. Similarly, I remember leaving Sighet for Auschwitz, the train that was about to take us there, but not much of what happened in the train itself. Bits of memory come back, but they do not add up to a consistent, continuous flow of events.

Many survivors report the opposite. They may not remember what happened yesterday but they claim that they remember vividly and with great detail every appearance, every event in Auschwitz fifty years ago. I can explain this rather strange phenomenon only in terms of my tendency to become panicky. I lost the ability to remember what happened when I was already on the train or in Auschwitz, not before and not after; only when the threat was real. I was overwhelmed and panic-stricken (less on the train than in Auschwitz) and my mind went blank. I must have functioned, participated in activities while I was there—otherwise I would not have survived—but no recallable trace was left. It was not recorded, and if it was recorded, it was not carried through the proper synapses. It remained buried. The subconscious locked it deeply in its interior, inaccessible to normal recall, and I have no desire to coerce its release.

THERE IS another respect in which I am different from many other survivors. Many survivors seized the first opportunity they encountered to return to the place of torture. They invited as many people as possible—friends, acquaintances, particularly children or grandchildren—to show them the arena of their suffering, where they wrestled with the Angel of Death and overcame him. I had opportunities to go back to Auschwitz and to Sighet and did not seize them. In 1975 I was in Russia, passed by Poland, and did not make the detour to Auschwitz. A few years later, my fellow Sigheter Moshe Scharf invited me to go with him to Sighet and I did not avail myself of this invitation. I have not yet been back to Auschwitz or Sighet. I am apparently subconsciously afraid to tread again the ground through which all hell broke loose underneath me. In my thoughts I morbidly dwell there; physically, however, I shun it. I dare not subject my body to the old rhythm of destruction.

―――

I AM easily wounded by abuse. I may show no reaction, but it takes its toll and I react inwardly. If I am walking and the pigeons disperse because of my approach, I feel bad. I do not like to scare anybody, any being; any scare is contagious. If I scare others I end up being scared myself.

I am also given to excessive fear, which I may have inherited from Grandfather. Where others see little peril, I perceive real threats. In camp, I was one of the very few people who always had to have bread (or whatever it was). I did not finish the old bread until the new bread had been distributed, thus subjecting myself to theft and danger. The bread often disappeared. But I needed the assurance that I would not starve to death. Keeping the bread gave me that assurance, while to others who were less fearful by nature it was more important to satisfy their hunger with an entire piece, all at once, than to have that psychological assurance. To this day, when the meal served in a hotel is free, my plate will be fuller than I can eat. My poverty of old cannot resist free food even when I do not need it.

My excessive fear, however, is directed mostly to human mischief or deterioration of health. I am less afraid of natural calamities such as thunder, lightning, or earthquakes, which makes me believe that the source of my fear is my encounter with human evil during the period of my incarceration in the ghetto and the concentration camps. I do not remember having this fear prior to this terrible period (although I must have had a propensity for it even then), whereas signs of meekness I can discern even before that period. I therefore assign their origins to different times—the first to conditions in my home, the second to the Holocaust period.

Let me also add that my fear is primarily of objects in the realm of the physical. Intellectually, I am considered bold, ready to defy convention with little inner contrition. When I first suggested my theory about the *stammaim*, the anonymous redactors of the Babylonian Talmud—about their non-contemporaneity with the authors whose texts they exposit, their not always having access to primary sources and therefore being vulnerable to offering wrong interpretations—I was told to desist and warned that I would be harshly criticized and condemned by those who hold more traditional views. Similarly, before I released a recent book concerning revelation, in which I embrace both the divine and the maculate nature of the Scriptures, a colleague advised me not to publish it in the present form, for I would be attacked mercilessly. I did not listen. I went through with my plans. Intellectually, I am more courageous. Jacob, in the Bible, feared Esau but wrestled with the Angel.

IN MY studies of the Talmud, I belong to a minority of Talmud scholars who can be characterized as text-immanent scholars; that is, their major activity is with the text itself: its development, evolution, transmission, its different components and how they were put together, whether they fit. We also study the relationship between the different Talmudic books, their purpose and mode of editing. All remains within the Talmudic milieu, and only rarely do we venture out of it to refer to the outside world, regarding the general culture in which these books took shape, or to engage in philological exchanges.

The majority of modern Talmud scholars are comparative scholars, whose aim is to show how much outside culture the Jews knew and incorporated in their texts, how many statements in the Talmud can best be understood if projected against similar backgrounds taking place outside the Jewish milieu. These scholars, however, usually do not study the Talmud in great depth (Professor Lieberman being a notable exception). In-depth study does not lend itself to parallelism. In order to look for parallels outside your own culture, your own system of thought, you have to deal with relatively superficial aspects of life. Superficially we all share many things; deep down we are different. Also, these scholars are interested only in one direction of influence: how much Greek, Roman, and Arabic cultures influenced Judaism. There was no flow in the opposite direction. Judaism did not influence Greek or Roman civilization or Arabic culture prior to Islam. This kind of study induces a sense of inferiority.

Professor Saul Lieberman, who wrote definitive articles and books about the influence of Hellenism and Greek culture in or on Jewish circles in the land of Israel, was possibly the greatest comparative Talmud scholar of all time. I started out that way when I came to study with him in 1954. I thought: I'll do what he's doing, and I prepared myself for it. I studied Greek and Latin, but three years later I stepped out of it and became absorbed in the text-immanent studies, in the Talmudic text itself. This decision made me also become more involved in the legal aspect of the Talmud, the halakhah. The comparative method deals primarily with the non-legal aspect of the Talmud, the *aggadah*. Aggadah, which consists of story-telling, aphorisms, and the like, has greater affinity with the outside world than does halakhah. Jewish law is unique.

I first thought that my choice of scholarly direction was due to my having had an intensive Jewish background—at the age of eighteen I could hardly read any non-Jewish book—and to my having begun my Talmudic studies at the tender age of five. This, I reasoned, made me remain within the confines of Jewish learning rather than stepping out into the almost hostile non-Jewish arena of studies. Now I do not think that this is the right explanation. Many other scholars came from similar intense backgrounds and experienced similar effects on their lives, and they not only adopted the comparative method but almost carried it as a kind of badge, to show that they had outgrown their infancy and environment and were now partaking of the world at large, that they were not to be identified with the old-fashioned scholars who, in the shtetl, in the small towns of Europe, studied the traditional way. Other people shared my background but were proud of their comparative excursions.

I now think there is a different explanation for my own direction. Although many of the comparative scholars shared my sort of education, and I shared their longing for knowledge of the wider world, they did not share in an extra psychological component: while I lived in Grandfather's house, where there were material hardship and health problems and the stigma of unmarried daughters, study became a crutch that helped me bear those adversities and, if not overcome them, at least live with them. That identity, that affinity between security and learning Talmud, may not have been shared by other scholars, and it may partially explain why I, and not many others, remained within Jewish learning, venturing only very rarely into the non-Jewish intellectual sphere. That sphere threatens my security. I consider myself versatile in various areas of scholarship, especially when their content impinges on the Jewish religion and its background. I believe that I am knowledgeable and erudite, as long as the knowledge is connected in some way to Jewish concerns. I am conversant with the background of scholars of all types who were Jews or who touched on Jewish subjects. My second field of interest is nineteenth-century *Chochmat Yisrael* (Jewish science), the relationship between its proponents and their activities. I am narrowly within the Jewish experience, even though not exclusively in the religious sphere. Being outside the Jewish experience apparently frightens me. Subconsciously, at least, that made me abandon the comparative method.

Perhaps it was not only my Jewish background but my Holocaust experience. Stepping out of the Jewish world conjures up an association that is painful and traumatizing. I live among non-Jews, and many of my friends and colleagues are non-Jews. For a decade I have been a professor at Columbia University, where I have shared respect and goodwill with many Gentile colleagues. Nevertheless, my experience made me different, and if I had embedded myself totally in non-Jewish scholarship, it might have been too painful.

ALTHOUGH PROFESSOR Lieberman was associated with the Jewish Theological Seminary, I didn't go to the Seminary soon after meeting him. I could not, because I had no secular knowledge. I had to start with elementary school. I went to elementary school for a semester and to high school for two years, until I was admitted to Brooklyn College, during which time I lived and learned in a yeshiva. Though I did not go to the Seminary then, I kept up the contact with Professor Lieberman, and several times a year I used to see him and speak with him. I subsequently also learned that Professor Lieberman signed the requisite papers guaranteeing that I would not become a public charge. This was necessary to enable me to stay in New York and to go to yeshiva there, rather than being sent to some other place in the country for adoption, as originally planned.

I came to Yeshivat Rav Chaim Berlin because of a cousin who preceded me to America and lived in the neighborhood of the yeshiva. He also contacted the veteran founder of the yeshiva movement in America, Rabbi F. Mendelowitz of Yeshiva Torah VoDaath, who in turn arranged a meeting with his two most senior teachers, ostensibly to have me join that yeshiva. The meeting with the senior teachers was unpleasant. I found them insensitive to my recent experiences. They asked me questions as though I had just stepped out of the beis medrash, and this was in February of 1947. (I cannot imagine that they treated me so insensitively because, as some people suggested afterward, they feared competition; I was, after all, a sort of landsman of Rabbi Mendelowitz.) Nevertheless, Rabbi Mendelowitz invited me to join his new *kollel* (a school for advanced Talmud study) in Spring Valley, New

York. It may very well have been the first such kollel in America. He even suggested by name a *chavruta*, a learning mate, with whom a study relationship would be fruitful.

My first reaction was "Will I be able to study secular subjects?" He looked at me, bewildered. "Secular education in a kollel?" A kollel shuns even non-Talmudic Jewish subjects. I politely declined. Whenever I recall this story, I feel a sense of ingratitude. He wanted to honor me with the highest level of Torah recognition for a yeshiva student, and I rejected it for what must have appeared to him a petty, if not blasphemous, reason. It did, however, further strengthen my resolve to join a yeshiva only if it allowed me simultaneously to study secular subjects.

ULTIMATELY, I became disillusioned with learning in the yeshiva. They treated me very well and I am eternally grateful to them. This was the only way that I could become acquainted with the Lithuanian style of yeshiva learning, and for a while I tried to excel at it. But I was disillusioned with its method of study, the yeshiva style, which I found too pilpulistic, too casuistic. I don't mean that description to be necessarily negative; its style is imaginative and fanciful and has enormous drawing power. It makes contradictions consistent with one another and finds no fault in any of the past sayings.

What distracted me from the yeshiva method—modern literary theory notwithstanding—was the paucity of authentic attempts to find out the original meaning of the author, the "authorial intention." On top of that, Talmudic studies in the yeshiva were often grafted onto kabbalistic knowledge. Later I learned that this amalgamation is based on the thought of the Maharal, the sixteenth-century sage of Prague, to whom the legend of the golem is attributed. Let me cite one example. It concerns the many places in the Talmud that say, "There is a lacuna in the text [of the Mishnah], and it should be read differently." In the eyes of a modern scholar, this Talmudic argument does major violence to the integrity of the Mishnaic text. The Maharal believed that because the Oral Law was not supposed to be written down, the compiler of the Mishnah intentionally, knowingly, omitted certain words in order to circumvent the original prohibition. This sort of apology struck me as very artificial. (Beyond the implausibility of the notion that someone would intentionally leave out essential information in order to circumvent the interdiction against writing, there is convincing evidence that during the second century, at the time that the Mishnah was compiled, the "Oral Law" was still oral, and it was not put into writing until centuries later.) I decided to leave, but reluctantly.

PERHAPS AN example, technical though it may be, may help to illustrate the differences between the three major approaches to the study of Talmud—the standard traditional method, the pilpulistic method, and the critical method—and will also clarify the significance of my own move to critical scholarship. The reader will note that, aside from technical, methodological differences, the critical approach is less respectful of long-held opinions— and, as a result, some people will never follow it, for it will offend their deference to that which is old and venerated. Thus, the shift toward the critical method does involve some adjustment—minor, I trust—in religious orientation.

This example is taken from the first mishnah of the Tractate *Kiddushin*, a tractate that outlines the Jewish laws of betrothal and marriage. The mishnah in *Kiddushin* opens with the statement "By three means a woman is acquired [in marriage]: by money, or by writ, or by intercourse; and by two means she acquires her freedom: by a bill of divorce, or by the death of her husband." The Babylonian Talmud, in its corresponding tractate, commenting upon this mishnah, inquires after the meaning of the mishnah's passive wording: "Let the mishnah state 'A man acquires a woman by three means [rather than "a woman is acquired"].'" The Talmud then explains: had the mishnah stated that "a man acquires a woman," one might draw the conclusion that he is able to do so against the woman's will. The phrase "a woman is acquired," the Talmud explains, implies that she is acquired only by her own consent, and not without it. This explanation troubled the medieval commentators, for the first mishnah in the second chapter of *Kiddushin* begins: "A man may betroth a woman either by his own act or by that of an agent." Here there is no passive wording, and therefore this latter mishnah, according to the Talmud's reasoning in the first chapter, seems to suggest that a woman may be betrothed against her will, which is not the case.

The Tosafot of the thirteenth century—the most influential glosses on the Talmud—defend the Talmud's explanation for the passive formulation in the Mishnah's first chapter by suggesting that since the proper conclusion is already implicit in the wording of the first chapter, the

Mishnah's second chapter is not concerned with the possibility of suggesting a wrong conclusion about the woman's own will. Since the first mishnah was careful to state "a woman is acquired," rather than "a man acquires," implying that the woman must consent, the second chapter could be less careful in its wording.

I wonder whether the Tosafists would have reached this explanation on their own had they not been obliged to defend the exposition of the Talmud. I call the interpretive manner of the Tosafists and of their colleagues and heirs the standard traditional method, and this method of reconciling passages in the Talmud was followed for generations.

A more involved and casuistic approach to interpreting Talmudic passages is known as pilpul. A pilpulistic manner (and there are many) of defending the Talmud's explanation of the mishnah's wording—if the pilpul came from a source close to the conceptual thinking popular in Lithuanian yeshivot—would probably center on drawing a distinction between "acquiring" and "betrothing." The first mishnah uses the language of acquisition, which has a coercive ring to it, while the second mishnah speaks of betrothal, which does not carry the same implications.

In Sighet, I heard another pilpulistic interpretation which is more typical of the rigors of this kind of learning. Rabbi Ezekiel Landau (1713–1793), in his famous book of responsa *Noda Beyehudah*, compares this case of betrothal to another case of agency in order to comment on this same question of the woman's free will. How, he asks, can the mishnah in the second chapter state that a man may betroth a woman through an agent when the law elsewhere says that a man cannot send an agent to collect money from a debtor who owes money to several creditors but has assets sufficient to repay only one? The agent cannot collect the money from the debtor if, by so doing, he precludes payment to the debtor's other creditors. How then, Rabbi Landau asks, can a man betroth a woman through an agent when, in doing so, he precludes other men from marrying her? Rabbi Landau answers that a woman cannot, after all, be compared to a debtor in this connection. A debtor is obliged to pay against his will, while a woman cannot be betrothed without her own consent. By accepting betrothal through the agent, the woman indicates her own choice of one particular man and becomes unavailable to others. No other man can lay claim to her, whereas a debtor remains in debt to his other creditors even when he repays one of them. By collecting repayment through his agent, a creditor potentially harms other creditors; but by betrothing a woman, with her consent, through an agent, a man can do no harm, since there can be no other legitimate claims upon her.

According to this pilpulistic argument, the fact that the mishnah in the second chapter says that a man may betroth a woman through an agent in itself suggests that a woman cannot be betrothed against her will. The betrothal through an agent must involve the woman's consent in order to be dissimilar from the prohibited collection of debts through an agent. The mishnah therefore has no reason to be concerned about suggesting the wrong conclusion, that a man can betroth a woman against her will.

All of these traditional explanations, conventional and pilpulistic, defend the Talmud's explanation of the difference in wording between the two Mishnaic chapters. The wording of the first chapter, according to these explanations, must indicate that a woman's consent is necessary for betrothal; but this is not necessary in the second chapter, either because of context or because the point has already been established. The critical method, however, will question the Talmudic assumption that the difference between "a woman is acquired" and "a man may betroth a woman" has to do with consent. The expression "a woman is acquired," in the first chapter, is, according to the critical method, a stylistic formulation and no more, consistent with the rest of that mishnah ("and . . . she acquires her freedom"). As to the mishnah in the second chapter, it stems from a different source; the Mishnah is compiled from different sources, dating from different periods. The word *mekadesh* ("sanctify"), used in the second chapter to indicate betrothal, is a Rabbinic term, whereas the "acquisition" of the first chapter is a biblical formulation (cf Ruth 4:10). The mishnah of the first chapter is older than that of the second chapter (which can be proved by other evidence, requiring a much longer technical discussion). The mishnah of the second chapter was composed by a different and later author, employing a different style and different terms.

Thus, traditional methods of study account for the different expressions by proposing meanings that are not apparent in the words themselves, while critical methodology reveals historical reasons for the discrepancy.

I SHOULD mention parenthetically that the opposition within the yeshivot to scientific textual study was not nearly as fierce fifty years ago as it is today. Then yeshivot were more tolerant of critical study (one can see this in the journals sponsored by yeshivot of the time), although they did not practice such scholarship themselves or train students to do so.

Yeshiva scholars were always interested in the meaning (practical or logical) of the sayings in the Talmud—the sayings themselves were taken for granted. Critical scholars are interested in the history of the text (to criticize, etymologically, means to judge, and the scholars judge the historicity of the text), and these scholars may be divided into two camps: those interested in the historicity of the facts cited in the Talmud, and those, among whom I hope I have made a substantial contribution, who are interested in the historicity of the sayings themselves: were they really said, by those to whom they are attributed, and in what form? It is difficult to ascertain which of the two scientific activities was more tolerated in the yeshiva circles. This probably differed from period to period. Still, questioning the authenticity of Talmudic sayings may be less acceptable to religious sensibilities, and hence less prevalent in yeshiva circles.

FOR YEARS after I left the yeshiva I carried in my wallet a piece of paper, until it was worn to shreds, which contained a note written by the rosh yeshiva, Rav Yitzhak Hutner, around 1949, before Passover. In it he authorized me to buy myself at his expense a suit and shoes in honor of the holiday. I had no income. It did not occur to me to go to work and earn money, even in the summer. I was too "European" for that. I ate and slept in the dormitory of the yeshiva and had no pocket money. When I arrived in 1947, some old ladies from the yeshiva's ladies' auxiliary used to stick a few dollars in my pocket, but they soon stopped. The old ladies died, and I had no money to buy myself clothes. Rav Hutner was aware of this and in a gracious manner alleviated my plight. (After 1950, Rabbi and Mrs. Aaron Wertheim took care of all my incidental needs and provided a second home for me.)

Rav Hutner also saw to it that I was socially comfortable in the yeshiva, which had very few refugee students. I had many private conversations with him, and they were always pleasant. During one of these conversations he once told me that he could teach me "something which nobody else can," and without his having named it, it was clear to me that he was referring to his *Mussar Shmussen*—literally, "ethical talks," but in fact they were more in the nature of theological talks. The Mussar Shmussen were considered by many to be the pride of the yeshiva. Rav Hutner inherited and further developed semi-mystical interpretations of biblical and Rabbinic texts, which he presented in a conceptual framework resembling a shiur, but which was delivered not as a lecture but as a talk with emotional overtones. Unfortunately, I was not attracted by the emotional quality of the talks and did not share the mystical suppositions accompanying them. I was already a philosophy major and later took a master's degree in theological philosophy. My taste in philosophy was and remained traditionally Western. So I saw only the holes and not the cheese in these talks, only the distortion of the plain meaning of the texts, which to me was unacceptable, and I decided I was going to leave.

As far as religious observance was concerned, I was

quite comfortable in the yeshiva. No amount of religious observance, no matter how strict or extreme, offends me. What offends me is intellectual violation. When I left the yeshiva in 1953–54 and went to study with Professor Lieberman at the Jewish Theological Seminary, I stayed there for thirty years. When I left the Seminary in 1985, it was the reverse. Intellectually, I was very happy there. I studied and taught the way the teachers there did, scientifically and critically. But I left for religious reasons. I was uncomfortable with their not always following the dictates and tenets that halakhah imposes on us as Jews.

HOW CAN one reconcile the two, the critical study, the intellectual perception of a text, and the adherence to strict observance, believing in the divinity of the text? This is a subject I try to deal with in the last chapter of my book *Peshat and Derash: Plain and Applied Meaning in Rabbinic Exegesis*, and in another book dealing with classical Jewish hermeneutics. However, my position—which is epitomized by my leaving the yeshiva because it was intellectually stifling and later leaving the Seminary because it was religiously wanting—is apparently difficult to follow. I seem to live with this combination in a certain amount of harmony. Will others follow suit? I often wonder whether I will succeed in transmitting this position to future generations, or whether it is not unique to my own particular intense Jewish background and people who do not share my background will experience tension that they will not be able to withstand. They will tend to follow either the religious side or the intellectual side, but not both.

I face a similar dilemma concerning my method of studying Talmud. The method needs to be divided into three steps. The first is to learn the text the way it is traditionally understood, with the earlier and later commentators, which many students can do. The second step is to stand back and ponder whether the interpretation offered by the commentaries is satisfactory or whether it is forced, put together in a manner that does not fit. This, too, I think, I can train students to perceive. The third step in the method is necessary if the commentaries prove to be forced, if the interpretations are not satisfactory, if the pieces of the text do not fit. If this is so, it is because sometime in the past an element of the text was mistransmitted or problematically arranged. Then all the pieces need to be reassembled differently from the way they were before.

This last step, which is highly intuitive, I find difficult to train students to master. They may get close to it but always fall short. This step may be summarized as saying, "Serious exegetical difficulties are often the result of compositional peculiarities." It is the hallmark of my method, and for students not to be able to duplicate it constitutes a personal setback for me. This has made me wonder whether my method is not due to something in myself that makes it difficult to transmit.

My doubts are even greater in the religious sphere, concerning the combination of "genuine faith and open-mindedness" (the motto of a newly founded rabbinical school, the Institute of Traditional Judaism, which I hope and pray will perpetuate the ideas that I am so ardent about. Intellectually, I am almost indistinguishable from a secular scholar, but, unlike one, I still believe in the holy nature of the Bible, believe that God broke into human history, and feel that religious observance is the best way for a person to approach God. A divine text, made maculate by men, is still divine and leaves no alternative but to seek, search, and peruse the maculate document for information on how to live a sacred life. I have often asked myself whether this particular combination, as I live it, has a chance to become more widespread. I often think of Moses Mendelssohn, who combined enlightenment with strict observance, apparently to his full satisfaction. I don't detect any tension in his writings. But he was a total failure with his children. They could not find his harmony, and broke away. So I wonder whether this kind of holding on to both things fervently, passionately, will find adherents, or whether it is something that is inseparable from my own intense Jewish commitment.

Concomitantly, from early childhood I combined devotion to scholarship *ki'pshuto*—study according to the literal meaning, not reading in and not reading out, which is the basis of scientific, critical study—with intense Jewish living. This combination seems to have been a mark of mine very early. Does it make me unique? I hope not. I prefer to believe that the method I champion is objective enough that people who will come after me—religious people—will want to embrace it, to emulate it.

6

REVERBERATIONS
In Retrospect

IT must have been with tongue in cheek that the great second-century sage of the land of Israel, Rabbi Shimon ben Yochai, speaking on a different matter, said, "Four things the Holy One, blessed be He, detests, and I don't like them either" (Babylonian Talmud, Tractate *Niddah* 16b). I would like to say the same, in all seriousness, in connection with the Shoah. There are four things that the Holy One, blessed be He, detests (at least this is my hope), and I reject them as well. These four things are, first, theological justifications of the Holocaust, which must be rejected out of hand; second, even raising the theological question of why there was a Holocaust, implying that an answer might be found; third, the notion that survival was possible only at the expense of others and that, therefore, every survivor must have a sense of guilt; and fourth, the idea that all survivors of the Holocaust necessarily share certain sociological and psychological characteristics. (In this last instance, unlike the first three, I merely disagree.

I would not go so far as to say that I detest those who search for commonalities.)

OF THE four things I have named, let me speak first of the one that I reject with derision: the attempt to make theological excuses for the Holocaust. I consider it obscene to assume that the Shoah took place (especially since it came from Germany) as a divine response to the spread of the German culture of Haskalah, or secularism, among the Jews. First of all, these apologies are historically absurd: Germany had the most secular Jews, and yet more Jews of other nationalities were exterminated. But, more important, these rationalizations are theologically offensive. The phrase "For our sins, we were exiled . . ." has a legitimate place in our tradition and liturgy; but dispersion, even with its attendant sufferings, is one thing, and vast annihilation of man, woman, and child is another. To say to people whom we know, "because of our sins" we were sent to Auschwitz—this must be rejected out of hand. There are certain times in history when justification almost smacks of participation. A justification, by definition, means: it should have happened, it's justice, it is the fitting course of events. People who make such statements suggest, in effect, that had it not happened, they would have worked to bring it about. Even aside from the historical absurdity, sensitive human beings must consider this abominable.

I WOULD go even further: not only is justification itself abominable; even raising the theological question of why there was a Holocaust—implying that there exists a satisfying answer—is objectionable. One should be encouraged to describe the enormity of the crime, its details and its comprehensiveness. One can also explain how it was possible, in the midst of the "bright light" of European culture, to commit such unspeakable atrocities. But one ought not, indeed one should not dare, to explain why it took place, why it happened as it did. For by merely asking the question "Why was there a Holocaust?"—implying that there is an answer, a just answer—one increases the suffering of the victims. Whatever the suggested answer might be—aside from the tautological statement that the perpetrators were wicked and that God "hid His face" and allowed things to occur—it will inevitably relieve the murderers, at least partially, of their guilt and place it upon the shoulders of the victims.

There are events in history, such as Revelation to the believer, that exist without explanation; they just exist. They have no "because." The Holocaust should be treated as such an event—an event without explanation. The repetition of the question "Why was there a Revelation?" causes pain to no one, though who can find an answer? The repetition of the question "Why was there a Holocaust," although no more answerable, causes pain to the victims. The question justifies their suffering. The very question reduces the innocence of the victims and the culpability of the murderers. The question should remain unasked.

Let us pursue every detail, every lead, every avenue that describes the horror and the tragedy—explicit information about how and where and who the victims were, how the evil was performed, how the crime was executed, how the atrocity came to fruition. The logistics of how it was possible to deceive such a large number of people and force them to their death, how it was possible to slaughter millions of people, should be explained. Everything that is knowable about the actual facts of the destruction should be researched and brought to public attention. All the cruelty, the indescribable torture and suffering, should become public knowledge.

But when it comes to explanations, we should be careful, lest we justify what happened. Sometimes the line between explanation and justification is very thin. Any logical explanation will accuse the victim, create a burden of guilt, and add to the victim's suffering. The very suffering is that we don't know why we suffered, we can't explain it, we can't conceivably say that God wanted children to be gassed. We can't attribute that to God; nor can we attribute it to sin, even though we believe that everything comes from God.

The Bible tells us that when Moses asked God, "I pray Thee, if I have found grace in Thy sight, show me now Thy ways, that I may know Thee, to the end that I may find grace in Thy sight," God obliged him and said, "My presence shall go with thee, and I will give thee rest." But when Moses asked God, "Show me, I pray Thee, Thy glory"—that is, God's honor, His being, His secrets—God rejected him, saying, "Thou canst not see My face, for man shall not see Me and live" (Exodus 33:13, 14, 18, 20). One can know God's ways but not God's reasons. So it is incumbent upon us to know every nuance of the suffering; but in the end, it must remain suspended in mystery. There is no explanation.

I appeal to philosophers, psychologists, and theologians to resist their tendency to find the root cause, to seek the rationale for the Holocaust. It is a unique event. They should not exercise their inclination to make it a link in a chain, part of a causal relationship. I am making this plea against raising the question of why there was a Holocaust even though, or because, I am, in principle, against literary censorship. I am opposed to any kind of suppression of historical study. No aspect of history should be declared off limits to research. Perhaps because I am so insistent on absolute freedom of inquiry in all areas of intellectual endeavor, I plead for an exception in the case of the Holocaust. The Shoah is unique in human history. It ought to remain so in scholarship as well. The tragedy, the enormity, the systematization, the ideology, and above all the helplessness that accompanied the Holocaust make the Shoah unprecedented: there was nothing a Jew could do in the face of the Shoah, unlike other persecutions, to mitigate the death sentence. To be born a Jew meant to be born to be killed. Scholars ought to discipline themselves by refraining from asking a question that, by its very nature, tends to diminish the uniqueness of the event, the culpability of the perpetrators, and to increase the despair of the survivors.

THE THIRD notion I reject is the idea that every survivor must have a sense of moral guilt. The assumption is that the only way you could survive was by resorting to some act which was not quite ethical, or which was somehow not in line with the standards you ought to follow; and if you accept this assumption, then you must have survived at the expense of someone else. *"Lo mineh velo miktzato!"*—this is not so in whole or in part! I can say categorically that I do not feel guilty for having survived. I am grateful to Almighty God that I survived, and I do not feel that my survival impacted adversely on the life of anyone else. There was one instance in which I was given cigarettes to distribute and some of them did not reach their destination, but other than this I can think of nothing I did that caused anyone else any suffering. There were people, of course, who survived by all kinds of moral compromises, but I daresay most survivors of concentration camps have no reason at all to feel such guilt.

Here allow me to insert a parenthetical appeal on behalf of those few who survived the concentration camps themselves. I often feel uncomfortable, to the point of being annoyed, when people claim to be survivors who actually escaped the camps. Not that I begrudge them their claims. Obviously, if they make such claims they have a need for them, and God knows, by all normal standards, they suffered appallingly. Still, I want to specify that those who survived the camps themselves—Majdanek, Treblinka, Auschwitz—one can count them; these people survived on totally different terms from those who went to a foreign consulate in '38 to struggle for a visa. Even if the visa was first rejected, or they almost missed it, or perhaps if they had come one hour, one minute, one second later, they would not have escaped and would have been sent to the camps—theirs was a totally different experience.

I often say that anyone whose lungs absorbed, on the ramp, on the station platform of Auschwitz, the smoke effusing from the chimneys of the crematoria—those who looked, or could not look, in Mengele's face, when right and left meant death and life—these are different people who have known a different kind of abandonment. That's not knocking on the door and begging, "Give me a visa." There is a different story for those who walked those ramps. Marching down that short road from the train to the crematoria cannot be duplicated by any other experience, whether the victims were aware or not aware. In fact, I remember one man from Sighet who had somehow saved a bottle of schnapps, and when he arrived at the ramp he drank it and became intoxicated on the spot. He had the presence of mind to know what was about to happen, and he saved his bottle for this eventuality. Similarly, those older women who took their daughters' children with them in the selection so that at least one person would have the chance to survive—these people showed enormous personal orientation, and with this orientation comes the enormity of the abandonment.

So, in a sensitive understanding, we must make this distinction. Let the others write books, movies, plays, whatever helps. Hitler's evil hand reached Jews, and other people, in all kinds of ways, throughout the world. Other peoples tell similar stories—refugees tell them—and our age, unfortunately, is full of such stories; but survivors of the camps themselves are different people who have experienced a different transformation. I think that this, for the record, should be made clear.

FINALLY, COMING to the fourth of my objections, my rejection diminishes, and I stand to be corrected by those who have a keener eye and are better trained in the social sciences. Nevertheless, I have not noticed any special characteristic unique to the survivors, and this despite the unique experience. Second to my work in Talmud, I follow the literature of Holocaust survivors closely, and I have not discovered anything of a predictable nature so that one might say: He or she is a survivor, therefore such and such will be the case. Of course, most survivors were anxious to rebuild their families, to regain the recognition in society that they lost. There are not many academicians among the survivors. There are some—more than one might suspect—but still relatively few. Probably this is because those who survived were constrained, as I was, to start their secular studies anew, from the elementary level and in a new language. Still, I do not see a common stripe that one might say arises from being a survivor.

However, having said that, I still believe that a sensitive survivor—and particularly one who has the opportunity or the leisure to pursue intellectual activity—must work, should work, under the influence of mutually contradictory forces. A sensitive survivor must recognize that there was a collapse of norms. Everything we held dear, everything we thought must be, and everything we thought must be pursued turned to nought. The Shoah signifies that whatever one considered the pattern of life one should choose—the ideal standard—collapsed. And if you are sensitive, in the face of this collapse you must reexamine what you stood for. You can put it as a test: If not for the Shoah, what would you be doing? If the answer is, "The same," then know that this is wrong. If you were teaching literature, for example, that literature failed, betrayed you. Something must be changed. Something must be different, intellectually—cannot be the same, should not be the same. So somebody who studied Talmud before and studies Talmud after has this problem. Something must be different.

I remember, after I came to the United States, Moshe Meisels Amishai, the Hebrew philosopher, asked me, speaking in Yiddish, "Were you religious before the war?" and I said, "Yes, of course I was, I was a chasid." "Are you religious now?" he asked. I said, "Yes." And he said, "I understand those who were religious before and became irreligious after, and those who were irreligious before and became religious after. I can't understand those who were religious before and remain religious after. *Nothing happened?* Something must have changed."

On the other hand, the person who has survived, and has been wounded so deeply, needs that support, that holding-on-to, which only tradition can provide. "Though He slay me, yet will I trust in Him" (Job 13:15). You cannot imagine, even if you follow the literature, the sadism of which the Germans and their cohorts were capable. I keep on reading the literature, and now and then I still come across something that shocks even me. That mankind could sink so low and inflict this kind of violence upon children: one must react to this spiritually. And at the same time, one must seek spiritual solace.

Opposite forces bear upon the survivor. On the one hand, one must find fault with what happened, for if there is no fault, there is an indirect affirmation. If you continue doing now what you would have done before, then you are saying that nothing was wrong—and you do not relate to what happened. Not criticizing the past is being like those who justify, those whom I mentioned at the start of this chapter—the ones who know why. Knowing why is a statement of approval. On the other hand, if you acknowledge the wrong, then you run the risk of cutting off the branch upon which you rest. A sensitive theologian must work with both sides, for if you take away the tradition, too, you take away the branch upon which you were raised and nurtured, and then you really are uprooted without any basis, without any roots.

Therefore the struggle this person has is the struggle to do both: to find a way of criticizing tradition, but of holding steadfastly to it. Criticizing affirms that something went wrong—badly wrong, deeply wrong. Yet there must be something to come home to. A person must find comfort and consolation in tradition. However, something in that tradition must be different, or else we say implicitly that nothing happened.

Personally, I found this balance in the critical study of Jewish texts, in a combination of criticism and belief in the divine origin of the text. My studies often question the veracity of the text as we find it, and at the same time they aim to increase the dignity of this text by restoring earlier readings. There are many instances in which the Gemara rejects the opinion of a sage, concluding with such interjections as *kashya* (it remains difficult), or *tiyuvta* (it is refuted), or in which the Gemara designates the statement of a particular sage as *beduta* (invented without sound basis), or *beruta* (outside, not on the mark). By picking out these passages and interpreting them in a manner that reveals the original context and meaning of the sage's words, Talmud criticism can be said to restore the dignity of our sages of blessed memory. It restores the dignity of the text, which in turn bestows dignity upon its authors; but it does so at the expense of questioning traditional reliability.

I undertake critical studies of the Talmud, and at the same time the Talmud is my bastion which I can always come home to and find solace in. This contradiction is not unlike the one that began to bother me in childhood and still troubles me. Once I wrote: "How is one to explain the blatant contradiction between counting and upholding every word, every letter of the text, and at the same time boldly announcing, '*Chasora mechasra vehacha ketani*'— 'There is a lacuna in the text, and it should be read differently'?" The Rabbis had to lend divine power to the text to lend power to their defiance of it. A lacuna in a human text is of no religious significance. A lacuna in a divine text? That already smacks of heresy. The Rabbis of the Talmud tampered with the biblical text, frequently offered interpretations that ran counter to the integrity of it, and openly said: There is a lacuna in the Mishnah. When God once wanted to intervene in a Rabbinic dispute, the Rabbis boldly rejected His intervention, saying: The Torah is not in heaven; it now belongs to man and not to God. Man exercises, as it were, leverage over Him. Man controls His Torah.

Gaining hegemony over a text, but at the same time insisting that it is a divine text, represents another arena in which this contradiction is expressed: that tradition failed, and yet there is a need for right and wrong to be continuous. This contradiction is fought out in the interplay between God saying, "*Nitzchuni banai*"—my sons have done me proud in their defiance—and God being stern elsewhere and saying, "You cannot do this."

DIFFERENT PEOPLE—sensitive survivors—will have to find equivalents in their own fields, in their creative endeavors. We must somehow find room for acknowledging that something went awfully wrong—that nobody extended help, not even God Himself. It is said of the Berditchever that he once interpreted the verse *"Lo ta'asun* keyn *ladoshem elokecha,"* "Do not do *thus* with the Lord your God" (Deuteronomy 12:4), as referring to God Himself. He pointed out that *keyn* also means "right": "Keyn *benot Zelophehad dovrot"*: "The daughters of Zelophehad are right" (Numbers 27:7). So the Berditchever said, *"Lo ta'asun* keyn *ladoshem elokecha"*—don't justify Him, *don't make Him right.*

Nonetheless, as religious Jews, we have to know that without God there is no humanity. Life makes sense only if we are hooked on to something higher, something transcendent. It's like a trolley car, if you've ever been in a trolley car: you may think the conductor is in charge, but the power comes from above. "Walk humbly with the Lord thy God" (Micah 6:8)—like a child holding hands. *You must hold hands, and walk.* But this does not mean that you always have to say, particularly in remembrance of the Holocaust, "What You did was right." It was terribly wrong.

IN LIEU OF AN INDEX

THERE is no dearth of memoirs by survivors. Indeed, it has almost become a duty for any survivor who can hold a pen (or who can hire someone who can hold a pen) to write down his or her memoirs. Each of them —even the least felicitous writer whose content is the expected and whose style is drab—contributes some newness that increases our awareness of the cruelty of the Holocaust's perpetrators. The purpose of such accounts, generally, is to chronicle the sufferings of the writer—the crueler, the more worthy of chronicling. There seems to be an inner drive to record one's tribulations as a means of reliving them, especially when, as was the case with the Nazis, the intent of the tribulation was to eradicate, to wipe the victim and his people off the human register. Remembering the suffering then becomes an act of defiance, showing that the criminals failed, that the victim still exists, and that this existence is acknowledged and recognized.

The purpose of this memoir is to define myself spiritually in the light of the Holocaust (what an odd combination, "light" and "Holocaust"). My spiritual self is learning, learning Torah, the Bible and the Talmud, as a highly stimulating pursuit permeated with divinity. Therefore I do not dwell much on cruelties, though I experienced my share of them. I merely hint at them in a subdued manner. The only cruelty that asserts itself again and again in these recollections is the gassing. More than fifty years later, it still overwhelms my imagination that human beings were able to do this to other human beings, especially to children. Just think of a child whom you love, your own, a relative's, a friend's, and imagine pushing him or her into the gas chamber. What kind of a person could do that?

THIS MEMOIR follows the biblical style, in which the physical appearances of the heroes are usually omitted because they are irrelevant. We do not know whether Moses was tall or short, thin or heavy—an unpardonable omission in the Greek style of writing. We do not know these things because they are not relevant to Moses' role as an intermediary between God and His people. The Bible tells us that Moses was slow of speech, but this fact is important: it is Moses' pretext for not wanting to appear alone before Pharaoh. In this memoir as well, physical descriptions are few and far between. Aside from those facts which are essential to the account, a small number of descriptions set the physical scene in a rudimentary way and hint at the details beyond.

Not everything that is paramount in my life is recorded

here. Among the omissions are my three sons and their families. Only someone who was without family for as long as I was can appreciate, as I do, the joy and sense of completeness that a loving family can provide. Also absent in the preceding pages is my passionate concern for Israel, the land, its history and tradition. Only one who has suffered from anti-Semitism for so long and who imbibed the divine story of Israel with his mother's milk, as I did, can appreciate the meaning and the import of this old-new country. Any threat to its existence or natural development evokes pangs of deep-seated personal fears.

These, and other things, are not included in this memoir because they are not integral to the spiritual odyssey that is expressed in my learning. They did not contribute to my survival and were not instrumental in defining my spiritual self as did, and does, learning. It was learning that made my life as a child bearable, insulated me from what was happening in the ghetto, and reached symbolic heights with the bletl, the page of holy text in which the German guard wrapped his snack; and it was learning that allowed me to resume my life after the Holocaust and to enter academia.

No wonder that the two people mentioned the most in this memoir are my grandfather, who taught me in Sighet, and Professor Saul Lieberman, my teacher in America. I have deviated from their styles of learning, from Grandfather's after his death and from Professor Lieberman's while he was still alive, which caused some friction, though it was soon overcome. I am more inclined toward source criticism, which both shunned. Source criticism looks for discrepancies in the early transmission of a text to account for forced interpretation. Grandfather was not acquainted with such scholarship, *per se*, and Professor Lieberman was uncomfortable with it. Yet I remain deeply influenced by both of them. My learning would have been quite different were it not for them. Without Grandfather, I might not have dedicated my life to learning altogether. They share in my development, one before and the other after the cataclysm.

IN THE course of these fifty years, since the destruction of the Jews of Sighet, countless books, articles, essays, poems, drawings, even movies—all conceivable means of expression have been mobilized to ponder the imponderable: How was it possible for human beings to be so savage and cruel to one another, to condemn a whole people, young and old, toddlers and hoary heads, hale and infirm, to be tormented, tortured, killed through unimaginable modes of death, with maximum pain, solely because of the accident of their birth? This enormous literature attempts to find out whether the destruction of European Jewry was an eclipse of history or a periodical outburst expected to be repeated. Was the Holocaust a mere whim of history, or is its cruelty inherent in each one of us, bursting out whenever the artificial constraint is removed?

Without passing judgment on the resolution of the "How was it possible?" question, indeed, on the feasibility of answering such questions in general, may I by contrast say that comparatively much less attention has been devoted to how those who survived made it, how they overcame the powers of destruction and left enough of them behind to start a new life. And if you want to peruse these inquiries at greater depth, you may ask: Are the survivors to be credited for their own survival? Was their survival due to their own strength, physically, emotionally, and spiritually, or was it merely an accident, a combination of circumstances that a few were lucky enough to have survived?

I suspect that the question of how the survivors survived is more difficult to answer, making it less inviting to deal with. Humankind's tendency to cruelty may be explained in terms of a few principles, whereas survival of cruelty needs to be explained in terms of individual stamina. It requires as many answers as there are individual survivors, which makes the task impossible. To put it differently: whereas those who perished perished more or less the same way and for the same reasons, those who survived survived in their own ways and for their own reasons. The former is within the domain of scholarship. The latter defies scholarly capabilities.

But not the capabilities of the memoir writers. They can and should describe not only how they made it physically (after one reads a few memoirs, most of the rest fall into discernible patterns) but also what spiritual power drove them to continue, not to falter under the yoke of hopelessness and despair. It constitutes, as it were, the soul of surviving. And like the soul of the body, it can easily be missed or denied. When this happens, the *élan vital* of survival has been extinguished and the memoir is incomplete.

A HADRAN

IT is a custom among traditional Jewish scholars to con-
nect the content of the end of a book with its beginning. This is called a *hadran* (colloquially translated as
"We shall return to you, O book"). This tradition may
have stemmed from the nature of a classical book: to be
read and reread. Connecting the end with the beginning
makes the repeating seem more like a continuation than
a new beginning. I will follow this custom and attach
here a note pertaining to the first chapter, thus, in the
spirit of a hadran, linking the beginning and the end of
this memoir by the same theme: the destruction of my
family.

I BEGAN this book by describing my relationship with my
family, particularly with Grandfather, from the time I
came to Sighet to live with him until we were parted by
Josef Mengele. I concluded the first chapter with the part-

ing, even though Grandfather and Mother lived for at least two more hours before they were gassed, for what happened to them in the gas chamber must remain unrecorded. It is incumbent upon us to describe and recall, in great detail—microscopically, as it were—all that transpired in the gas chamber and en route to it, including the loss of control of natural human constraints and needs, in order to accentuate the enormity of the crime. When, however, the victims in question are one's own relatives and intimates, describing their last gasps in the gas chamber, even out of sympathy for them, would be a breach of privacy, an obscene voyeurism, exposing them, personally, in a position in which they do not wish to be seen.

To describe what happened to the anonymous victims in the gas chambers, the ghoulishness to which they were subjected, if it serves (and it always does) juridical and incriminatory purposes—by all means. But to describe what happened there to your mother, your grandfather, your neighbor whom you knew well—with all your good intentions of communing with their memory—will diminish your empathy with them, the basis of all commemoration. Commemoration is a form of identification with the person commemorated. That person must remain shrouded in honor and dignity and accessible to ordinary imagination. What cannot be imagined—and what happened in the gas chamber is unimaginable—cannot be commemorated.

But this does not prevent me from wanting to know how my mother and grandfather died. Were they among the first to enter the gas chamber, so that they probably died even before the gas was released, crushed by the weight of so many bodies on them; or were they among the last ones to enter, pushed in by the kapos, so that they may have died of suffocation before the SS injected the gas into the chamber; or were they among those who entered the gas chamber while it was not yet full, so that they had some time, seconds, for reflection? What were their thoughts? Did they think of me? They did not blame God. Their belief in God was total and unconditional. Did they blame the Jewish leaders for not warning them to escape? They were not that politically sophisticated. If they blamed anyone, it was only themselves for their own sins—they may have seen themselves as God's scapegoat —making their suffering so much greater.

GLOSSARY

Throughout this book the word "learning" is used in a sense slightly different from its common English usage. "Learning," in this book, is similar to the Yiddish *lernen*, which is used especially to denote the study of traditional subjects. When one Jew asks another, "What are you learning?" the question means, "What text and what issue are you currently studying?" In traditional Jewish circles, one does not "study," one *learns*.

aggadah   (Hebrew, from the root *negad*, "drawing, continuum") The non-legal parts of the Talmud and of other traditional texts. Aggadah may include edifying exhortations, anecdotes, metaphysical discussions, and history, among other topics. Aggadah stands in contrast to halakhah, legal material. Aggadah and halakhah are interwoven in the discussions of the Talmud. *See also* HALAKHAH.

agunot (sing. *agunah*; Hebrew: "those who are fettered") Women whose husbands have disappeared without the fact of their death being certain (often in battle or in enslavement), or have otherwise left them without first granting a bill of divorce. A woman in this situation cannot remarry until either the death of her husband is confirmed or he grants her a divorce. In Israel and in Western countries, a woman whose husband refuses to give her a *get* (a divorce) is also called an agunah.

angemachts (Yiddish) Fruit preserves, made of prunes, berries, and the like, and sugar, which are kept all year long, after the fruit season is over.

arba kanfos (Hebrew: "four corners") A name for the traditional fringed garment (also called a *tallit katan*, a "small tallis") worn by observant Jewish men during the daylight hours (in fulfillment of Numbers 15:37–41) so that the special tassels on the four corners of the garment (called *tzitzit*) may remind them of the Torah's commandments.

Bava Kama (Aramaic, the "First Gate") A tractate in the order of *Nezikin* ("Damages"). This tractate is followed by *Bava Metzia* and *Bava Batra* (the "Middle" and "Last" Gates). Children usually begin their Talmud study with either the second chapter of *Bava Metzia*, *Eilu Metziot*, which deals with lost objects, or with the third chapter, *Hamafkid*, which deals with bailees. Both subjects are assumed to be easily grasped by children. I started my Talmud study with *Hamafkid*. So did my middle son, Ephraim, who is also a Talmudist.

beduta,
beruta

(*Beduta*, Aramaic: "foolish, invented without sound basis"; *beruta*, Aramaic: "outside, not on the mark") Similar Talmudic expressions (often interchanged in variant readings of the same passage). These expressions indicate that the statement of a sage has been rejected as illogical or not sensible. There are, however, occasions in which statements rejected in the Talmud as beduta or beruta are nevertheless regarded as authoritative by later rabbis.

beis
medrash

(Yiddish, from Hebrew *beit midrash*: House of Study) A place (often doubling as a synagogue and library) in which students beyond the cheder level study traditional texts, individually and in chavruta, on their own and/or with the formal or informal guidance of teachers and others studying there. The common study hall of a yeshiva or kloiz may be called its beis medrash. *See also* CHAVRUTA; CHEDER; KLOIZ.

Berakhot

(Hebrew: "benedictions") A tractate of the Talmud in the order of *Zeraim* ("Seeds") that deals with the recitation of blessings.

Berditch-
ever, the

(1740–1810) Levi Yitzchak, the rabbi of Berditchev, a town in Poland. In popular lore and song he appears as one who defends the Jewish people and acts as an intercessor between them and God.

biber

(Yiddish, from German *Biber*: "beaver") The round hat worn by Satmarer chasidim, made of beaver fur.

chanukat habayit   (Hebrew: "housewarming" or "house dedication") In the Bible, the dedication (and rededication) of the Holy Temple (hence the holiday of Chanukah, in celebration of the Temple's rededication). Colloquially, a housewarming party.

chasidim   (sing. *chasid*; Hebrew: "righteous ones, pious ones") The word has identified several Jewish groups throughout history, but is used in this memoir in its current sense, exclusively in reference to members of the chasidic sects, adherents of rebbes whose tradition descends from Rabbi Israel Baal Shem Tov of the early eighteenth century. *See also* REBBE.

chasidut   (Hebrew) The practice of chasidism.

Chasora mechasra vehacha ketani   (Aramaic: "there is a lacuna [in the Mishnah], and it should be read as follows") A phrase employed by the sages of the Talmud when they feel that a passage in the Mishnah ought to be augmented or corrected. To modern, critical scholarship, such interventions appear to violate the Mishnah's integrity. Tradition, on the other hand, accounts for these emendations in other ways. One view holds that the emendations are meant only as elucidating accompaniments to the Mishnah's original wording, and another opinion suggests that because it was originally forbidden to write down the Oral Law, Rabbi Judah haNasi, Rabbi Judah the Prince, the Mishnah's compiler, intentionally omitted certain words and phrases so as not to violate this prohibition absolutely (although in fact there are also a few places in the Talmud where this phrase is applied to a non-Mishnaic source).

GLOSSARY

chavruta   (Aramaic: "companionship") In traditional Jewish study, the word denotes a study partner or partnership.

cheder   (Hebrew: "room") An elementary religious school (often held in a small room) for children in their early, formative years. More mature students continue their studies in a yeshiva.

chevra kadisha   (Hebrew, "holy society") The burial society, those who arrange burials and prepare bodies for interment.

chiddush   (Hebrew: "innovation") Used here, and in traditional Jewish study, to denote a new twist in the understanding of a text.

Chochmat Yisrael   (Hebrew: "wisdom of Israel") The term is used in a text dating back to the second century, where it refers to the study of Torah in all its ramifications. Here it is used to denote the nineteenth-century "science of Judaism" in which modern critical methods were brought to bear on Jewish history and text.

Chol Hamoed   (Hebrew: "the profane [days] of the [sacred] time") The intermediate days of a festival, between its opening and closing sabbatical days. During Chol Hamoed, certain sorts of day-to-day work (including the carrying of money) are permitted, while certain restrictions and festive commemorations of the holiday remain in effect (the eating of unleavened bread during Passover, and dwelling in booths during Sukkot, for example).

chosen   (Yiddish, from Hebrew *chatan*) Bridegroom. In the Bible, the word also denotes a daughter's husband.

Chulin   (Mishnaic Hebrew: "profane, not holy") A tractate of the Talmud in the order of *Kodashim* ("Hallowed Things") that deals especially with the laws of ritual slaughter.

Chumash   (Hebrew, from *chamesh*: "five") The Pentateuch, the Five Books of Moses. The word is used particularly in Yiddish.

chupah   (Hebrew: "canopy, chamber, bridal chamber") Already in Rabbinic (though not in biblical) Hebrew, the word is used exclusively to denote the wedding canopy or chamber. Popularly, it refers to the ceremony conducted under the chupah.

daiges parnasa   (Yiddish pronunciation and usage of Hebrew, "concern for livelihood") Responsibility and concern for livelihood, especially that of a scholar.

dapim   (sing. *daf*; Hebrew: "planks"; in later usage, "leaves [of a book]") Folio pages, especially of Talmud. The two sides of a single page comprise one daf and are numbered, e.g., 2a and 2b respectively. To "learn a daf," therefore, is to study the two sides of a page of Talmud.

dayan   (pl. *dayanim*; Hebrew: "judge" [rabbinical]) A religious judge who is consulted primarily with regard to ritual matters.

dershrocke-
ner
(Yiddish, from German *erschrocken*: "fright-
ened") One who is given to fears; one who suffers
from irrational fears, but not to the extent that it
interferes with his normal life.

Dinah
(Hebrew) Jacob's daughter. Here she is mentioned
in connection with the events of Genesis 32–33.

d'var Torah
(pl. *divrei Torah*; Hebrew: "word [or matter] of
Torah") Denotes primarily a short sermon or ob-
servation on a biblical text.

Even Haezer
(Hebrew, "the Stone of Help" or "the Stone of
the Helper": I Samuel 4:1, 5:1, 7:12) The third
order of the *Shulchan Aruch*, dealing with the relationship between man and wife. The title was
probably first used by Rabbi Eliezer ben Natan of
Mainz (1090–1170; author of the book *Ravan*),
even (meaning "stone") being a Hebrew acronym
of his name. *See also* SHULCHAN ARUCH.

farfroirener
(Yiddish, from German *gefroren*: "frozen") One
who complains of cold when others do not feel
cold.

farher
(Yiddish, from German *Verhör*: "interrogation")
The testing of a young student through oral ques-
tioning to ascertain depth and breadth of learning.

frum
(Yiddish, from German *fromm*: "pious, believing") Religiously observant. ("The more *frum* one
is, the more . . .") One who observes the religious
laws and rituals is called a *frumer*.

gabai   (Hebrew) A Rabbinic term for one who collects
           taxes or charities. Colloquially, in Yiddish, the
           word came to denote one who takes care of a syn-
           agogue's affairs or those of a chasidic rebbe. *See
           also* REBBE.

geihinom   (Hebrew, from *gey hinom* [and *gey ben hinom*],
           "the Valley of Hinnom" mentioned many times in
           the Bible, the first time in Joshua 15:8) From Rab-
           binic literature onward: hell. In the Bible, a place
           where children were offered in idolatrous sacrifice
           to the god Molech.

Gemara   (Aramaic: "teaching") Similar in meaning to *Tal-
           mud* and *Mishnah*: all of these terms mean "teach-
           ing." The synonyms are used to denote different
           Rabbinic corpora. Technically, *Gemara* denotes
           the commentary of the Amoraim (scholars who
           flourished after the second century C.E.) on the
           Mishnah. The Mishnah and Gemara together
           comprise the Talmud. In practice, the terms *Ge-
           mara* and *Talmud* are used interchangeably. In
           teaching, I usually use *Gemara* in reference to the
           anonymous, editorial voice and material of the
           Talmud, which I hold to be the voice and contri-
           butions of the Talmud's fifth-century redactors.
           See also MISHNAH; TALMUD.

godel   (Yiddish, from Hebrew *gadol*: "great, a great
           man") One who has excelled in knowledge and in
           piety.

gut yom tov (Yiddish *gut* [from German]: "good," and Hebrew *yom*: "day," and *tov*: "good") A colloquial holiday greeting. There is a redundancy in this greeting, for the Yiddish word *gut* is synonymous with the Hebrew *tov*. However, the words *yom tov* together mean "holiday" in Hebrew, so the greeting may be translated "good holiday."

hadran (Aramaic and Hebrew) The word appears at the end of each tractate of the Talmud, with the word *'alach* ("upon you") and the name of the tractate (e.g., *hadran 'alach . . . Chulin*). The formula is widely and incorrectly translated from the Aramaic as "We shall return to you [O tractate]." The correct translation is from the Hebrew: "our beauty [or honor] upon you."

Häftlinge (German) Prisoners; here, prisoners of the concentration camps.

Hagigah (Hebrew: "celebration") A tractate of the Mishnah's second order, *Moed* ("Set Feasts"), which deals with festal offerings, among other topics.

halakhah (Hebrew) The legal material of the Talmud and of other Rabbinic texts. A single law is also termed a halakhah. Often the term appears in contradistinction to *aggadah*. *See also* AGGADAH.

ilui (Yiddish, from Hebrew) A young scholar who shows prodigious ability in the study of Talmud and related knowledge.

ivre	(Yiddish, from Hebrew *ivrit*: "Hebrew [language]") Facility and fluency in Hebrew reading.
kabbalat 'ol malkhut shamayim	(Hebrew: "acceptance of the yoke of the Kingdom of Heaven") Recognition of God as the Creator and the giver of the Torah.
kabbalat 'ol mitzvot	(Hebrew: "acceptance of the yoke of commandments") Recognition of the commandments as binding.
Kaddish	(Aramaic, cognate of Hebrew *kadosh*: "holy") The doxological prayer (almost entirely in Aramaic) recited between segments of the synagogue service and after sessions of study, and especially by mourners during a period of eleven months (among Ashkenazic Jews) following the death of a close relative and, thereafter, upon the anniversary of the death and during Yizkor, the memorial service. *See also* YIZKOR.
kal vachomer	(Hebrew: "light and strict") The first of the thirteen hermeneutic principles of Rabbi Ishmael, in the form of "If there is leniency in a more strict case, how much more should there be leniency in a less strict case." This principle is found already in the Bible itself, as when the brothers say to Joseph, "Behold, the money, which we found in our sacks' mouths, we brought back unto thee out of the land of Canaan; how then should we steal out of thy lord's house silver or gold?" (Genesis 44:8). This hermeneutic principle is one of the few still creatively employed in rabbinic writing today, many of the others being severely curtailed.

kapote   (Yiddish) A big caftan—not hooded—worn daily only by the more prominent male members of a chasidic community, relatives of the rebbe and scholars, and by almost all chasidic men on the Sabbath and on holidays. *See also* CHASIDIM; REBBE.

kashya   (Aramaic: "It remains difficult") Employed in the Talmud, according to a reliable tradition, whenever a problem concerning a sage's statement is noted but nevertheless does not cause the statement to be rejected. To respond to such difficulties, even though the Talmud leaves the issues unresolved, is considered religiously permissible by some. I know of at least one late-medieval book whose aim is precisely to resolve these problems. *See also* TIYUVTA.

Kazetnik   (Yiddish, from German *KZ* [*Konzentrationslager*]: "concentration camp") Inmate of a concentration camp.

Kever Yisrael   (Hebrew: "Israelite grave and/or burial") Jewish burial rites; the grave of a Jew (especially if among other Jews).

Kilayim   (Hebrew: "Diverse Kinds") The name of a tractate of the Mishnah in the order of *Zeraim* ("Seeds": agricultural laws). The tractate details and delimits the biblical prohibition against raising diverse plants together in one field or vineyard. *See also* MISHNAH.

ki'pshuto   (Aramaic: "According to its plain or contextual meaning") To study a text *ki'pshuto* is to study it according to the clear and usual meanings of its words and phrases, without recourse to excessively eisegetical interpretations or to interpretations that diverge from the plain meaning.

kloiz   (Yiddish) A less formal synagogue and/or place of study. When a group of chasidim following the same rebbe organized a synagogue or less formal *beis medrash*, they often called it the kloiz of their rebbe's sect (e.g., the Viznitser Kloiz, Belzer Kloiz). *See also* BEIS MEDRASH.

Kluger,   Rabbi Shloma Kluger, of Brody, Galicia (first half
Rabbi   of the nineteenth century). His commentary,
Shloma   though almost contemporary, was included in Pesil Balaban's comprehensive edition of the *Shulchan Aruch* and its major commentaries. *See also* SHULCHAN ARUCH.

kollel   (Hebrew, "comprehensive, inclusive"; by extension, a community of people from diverse places) In recent usage: a yeshiva of the highest level.

kols   (Yiddish, from Hebrew *Kahal*: "congregation,"
chadorim   and *chadarim*: "rooms") A community religious school of the elementary level. *See also* CHEDER.

kvitlach   (Yiddish) Pieces of paper upon which personal petitions are written and submitted to chasidic rebbes or placed at the grave sites of great rebbes (or in the crevices of the Western Wall in Jerusalem).

**Lo mineh
velo
miktzato**
(Aramaic) Talmudic expression meaning "It just isn't so!" Literally: "Not it itself and not part of it."

**Martyrs,
Ten**
The ten great Rabbinic sages and teachers (among them Rabbi Akiva) who, according to tradition, were condemned to martyrdom by the Roman emperor, ostensibly for the sin of Joseph's brothers, but more immediately for having taught Torah to their pupils in defiance of a royal edict.

mefalpel
See PILPUL.

Michael
(Hebrew) The angel Michael; according to tradition, the most beneficent of angels (see Daniel 12:1). Some Jews recite before going to sleep, "On my right [the angel] Michael, and on my left [the angel] Gabriel, and in front of me [the angel] Uriel, and behind me [the angel] Raphael, and above my head the presence of God."

Midrash
(Hebrew) An interpretation of a biblical text. The root *d'r'sh* means to "seek or ferret out." Here the word is used in the sense of seeking or ferreting out the implicit meaning of a text; it may refer to a corpus of Midrash or to a single interpretation.

mikveh
(Hebrew: "gathering of waters") In rabbinic Hebrew and in Yiddish, the ritual bath.

mi'sheberach

(Hebrew: "He Who Blessed") A prayer of supplication, named for its opening phrase—"May He Who blessed our fathers"—recited (during the portion of the synagogue service in which the Torah is read) for the benefit of an ailing person, or a woman having given birth, that they shall be healed, or for a person called to the Torah, that he shall prosper.

Mishnah

(pl. *mishnayot*; Hebrew: "teaching") Similar in meaning to *Gemara* and *Talmud*. The most authoritative Rabbinic text (anthologized by Rabbi Judah haNasi, Rabbi Judah the Prince, around 200 C.E.) The word may denote the entire corpus of the Mishnah, or any one segment of this text. *Also see* GEMARA; TALMUD.

mitnaged

(pl. *mitnagdim*: Hebrew, "the one who opposes") In contradistinction to chasid: a religious Jew who does not accept the teachings, traditions, and authority of Rebbe Israel Baal Shem Tov and his successors, the chasidic rebbes. *See also* CHASIDIM.

mitzvah

(Hebrew: "commandment") A commandment of the Torah. In popular usage, any good deed.

Musaf

(Hebrew: "addition") The additional synagogue service of a Sabbath or festival. *See also* VEHIKRAVTEM.

nachas

(Hebrew: "satisfaction") Hence the very popular Yiddish usage: the satisfaction or pride incurred through the accomplishments of a dependent.

Nasi   (Hebrew) During Mishnaic and Talmudic times: Patriarch. It is generally thought that the institution of the Patriarchate lasted until 425 C.E. in the land of Israel.

Netziv, the   Acronym for the famous nineteenth-century Rabbi Naftali Zvi Yehuda Berlin of Volozhin (1817–1893).

nitzolei   (Hebrew) Survivors of the Holocaust.
haShoah

ohel   (pl. *ohalim*; Hebrew: "tent") Here the word denotes a sheltering structure erected over the grave of a chasidic leader so that his followers may come and pray there.

Orach   (Hebrew, "The Way of Life") The first order of
Chaim   the *Shulchan Aruch*, dealing with daily rituals: prayer, Sabbath observance, etc. *See also* SHULCHAN ARUCH.

Oral Torah,   Jewish law and lore is divided into two parts: the
Written   "Written Law"—that is, the Holy Scriptures—
Torah   and the "Oral Law"—that body of law which was originally transmitted orally (the Midrash, Mishnah, and Gemara) and the commentaries pertaining to this corpus (as well as any tradition, considered "Torah," not included in the Scriptures).

189

Peri
Megadim

(Hebrew: "Luscious Fruits") The name of a book (whose title is based on the Song of Songs 4:13), written by Rabbi Joseph Teomim in the middle of the eighteenth century. In Sighet, one was required to know this book quite well for ordination.

peyos

(Hebrew: "earlocks") Many chasidim do not cut off this hair, in observance of Leviticus 19:27.

pilpul

(Hebrew) Argumentation; usually tortuous and/or casuistic argument. Used here in reference to the studying of a text not according to its plain or contextual meaning but in a convoluted way. A *mefalpel* is one who engages in pilpul. *See also* KI'PSHUTO.

Rambam

Acronym for Rabbi Moses ben Maimon (1135–1204), also called Maimonides—rabbi, physician, and philosopher; the greatest Jewish codifier of the Law and philosopher. Owning "a set of *Rambams*" means possessing all the volumes of his legal treatise, the *Mishneh Torah*.

Ran

(Hebrew) Acronym for Rabbenu Nisim son of Reuven from Gerona, Spain, one of the great Talmudists of the fourteenth century.

Rashi

Acronym for Rabbi Shlomo Yitzhaki (1040–1105), the premier commentator of the Middle Ages on the Bible and the Talmud, whose comments, to this day, are printed alongside both texts in traditional editions.

GLOSSARY

rebbe   A chasidic rabbi and leader, head of a chasidic sect, whose authority and stature derive from a dynastic lineage traced back to the first followers of Israel Baal Shem Tov.

rebetzin   (Yiddish) The wife of a rabbi.

Reishit Chochmah   (Hebrew: "the Beginning of Wisdom") A biblical phrase (Psalm 111:10, Proverbs 4:7) used by several authors as the title of their work.

rosh yeshiva   (pl. *rashei yeshivot*; from Hebrew *rosh*: "head," and *yeshiva*) The chief teacher of a yeshiva or, more recently, any teacher in a yeshiva.

Sayings of the Fathers   (From Hebrew *Pirkei Avot*) A tractate in the fourth order of the Mishnah, *Nezikin* ("Damages"). It is the sole tractate composed entirely of aphorisms attributed to the Mishnaic sages.

Shabbat   (Hebrew: "the Sabbath") A tractate of the Talmud's second order, *Moed* ("Set Feasts"), which deals with the proper observance of the Sabbath.

shaliach l'kidushin   (Hebrew: "messenger for betrothal") A technical, Talmudic term for a messenger sent to betroth a wife on behalf of someone else. If the messenger were to die before returning and revealing the identity of the chosen woman, the sender would be prohibited from marrying anyone because any woman might conceivably be a blood relative of his betrothed.

shaliach
l'shiduchin   (Hebrew: "messenger for matchmaking") A messenger sent to choose (but not betroth) a wife for someone else. If such a messenger were to die before returning and revealing the identity of the chosen woman, the sender would still be allowed to marry, since no betrothal was executed on his behalf.

sh'at
hadehak   (Hebrew, "hour of distress [or emergency]") Here, a reference to the Talmudic idiom for a time in which drastic measures may be taken, and drastic legal solutions sought to pressing religious problems. In sh'at hadehak, one might rely upon a Talmudic minority opinion even if it had previously been overruled.

shidduch   (Hebrew) A match; a matrimonial alliance.

shiur   (pl. *shiurim*; Hebrew) The word has many meanings. Here it is used in the sense of a lesson on a Talmudic or other legal text.

Shoah   (Hebrew) In the Bible (see Isaiah 47:11), "devastation, ruin." In modern Hebrew, a term for the Holocaust.

shochet   (Hebrew) One who slaughters animals according to the specific ritual requirements for preparing kosher meat.

shtiebel   (pl. *shtieblach*; Yiddish, from German *Stube*: "room") Small room used as a synagogue, usually in a private house, whose affairs are conducted by the congregants without a rabbi or a cantor.

shtreimel   (Yiddish) Sable fur hat, made of thirteen tails, worn by chasidim on the Sabbath and on holidays.

Shulchan Aruch   (Hebrew: "The Laid Table") The name given to the most authoritative book of Jewish Law.

siddur   (Hebrew, from *seder*: "order") A prayer book in which the prayers are arranged according to the daily (and special) services.

simanim   (Hebrew) Signs, marks—often as used to facilitate identification and memory.

stammaim   (from Aramaic *stama* and *stama degemara*: "closed, anonymous") A term that I coined to refer to the anonymous redactors of the Gemara whose connective remarks narrate the Talmud and hold it together. The *stammaim* flourished during the latter half of the fifth century in Babylonia.

sugya of Rabbi Chanina segan haKohanim   (Aramaic and Hebrew: "The Talmudic Discussion of Rabbi Chanina, the Priests' Deputy") The name given to fifteen pages of the Babylonian Talmud (Tractate *Pesachim*, 14a–21a), which deal with the laws of ritual purity (particularly in the Temple) and which are considered to comprise one of the most difficult passages of the Talmud. *Sugya*, in Babylonian Aramaic, means "spread, a distance, a walk" (and thence "a section" or "a discussion"), and *segan* is a biblical word for "prefect." The section begins with the words "Rabbi Chanina, the *segan* of the Priests, said . . ."

Ta'anit (Hebrew: "fast") The name of a tractate of the Talmud's second order, *Moed* ("Set Feasts"). It deals with how and when to proclaim a public fast.

talmidath chacham (Hebrew: "the [female] student of a sage") A feminine parallel to the idiomatic epithet *talmid chacham* ("[male] student of a sage"; pl. *talmidei chachamim*). The original idiom is used to denote a man who has become learned in traditional texts. As Jewish women achieve ever greater proficiency and experience in traditional study, a feminine version of the term becomes necessary.

Talmud (Hebrew: "teaching") Similar in meaning to *Gemara* and *Mishnah*: all of these terms mean "teaching." The Talmud is the most influential book (after the Scriptures) in Jewish religion. The Talmud consists of the Mishnah and the Gemara and was probably edited, although not completed, around the fifth century in Babylonia. *Talmud* often serves as a synonym for *Oral Law*, for much of it was transmitted orally for more than a millennium. *See also* GEMARA; MISHNAH; ORAL TORAH.

tashlich (Hebrew: "You will cast") A ritual of repentance in which Jews go to a (preferably) living body of water and empty crumbs from their pockets, symbolically evoking the verse "You will hurl all our sins into the depths of the sea"—a custom of late medieval origin.

tephilin   (Mishnaic Hebrew) Phylacteries worn by Jews during morning prayers and containing scriptural passages on parchments.

time-bound commandments   Traditionally, in Judaism, women have been exempted from time-bound commandments (ones that must be performed at a specific time), presumably because they are assumed to be busy with their family duties.

tish   (Yiddish, from German *Tisch*: "table") A communal meal conducted by a chasidic rebbe with his followers on the Sabbath or on a festival. Whoever attends a tish is generally assumed to be a follower of the presiding rebbe.

tiyuvta   (Aramaic: "It is a refutation") A Talmudic expression that indicates an effective refutation of a sage's statement. Once it is so refuted, no traditional scholar will reconsider the statement. Critical scholarship does not abide by this restriction and sometimes suggests that such statements were originally well founded, or valid in more original contexts. *See also* KASHYA.

Torah VoDaath   (Hebrew: "Torah and Wisdom") The name of a yeshiva in Brooklyn.

Torat imecha   (Hebrew: "the instruction of your mother") Used here with reference to the obligation to follow the customs of one's parents.

Tosafot   (Hebrew: "additions") Annotations to the Talmud
                by the great French and German medieval schol-
                ars of the twelfth to the fifteenth centuries.

Tzadik   (Hebrew, "righteous one, upright one") A fre-
                quent word in the Bible, here it is used in reference
                to a chasidic rebbe as perceived by his followers.

vehikravtem   (Hebrew, "And you shall offer . . .") The opening
                of a biblical verse that describes the sacrifices of-
                fered in the Temple on a given day. Such verses
                are repeated in the Musaf services of festivals in
                commemoration (and in lieu) of the Temple ser-
                vice. *See also* MUSAF.

Vilner Shas   (Yiddish: Vilnius, and Hebrew acronym for *shisha
                sedarim*: "six orders [of the Mishnah and Tal-
                mud]") The complete and most influential edition
                of the Babylonian Talmud, printed in Vilnius,
                Lithuania, in the second half of the nineteenth
                century. To this day it is considered the best edi-
                tion of the Talmud.

yahrzeit   (Yiddish, from German *Jahreszeit*: "season") The
                anniversary of a person's death, commemorated
                by close relatives with the recitation of the Kad-
                dish prayer. *See also* KADDISH.

yehudim   (Hebrew) Already, in the Bible, a name for the
                Jewish People. In Yiddish, the word is reserved for
                "uptown" assimilated German Jews.

GLOSSARY

Yerushalmi (Hebrew: "Jerusalemite") The Gemara of the land of Israel (in contradistinction to that of Babylonia), which was completed around the last quarter of the fourth century (not in Jerusalem). It is less studied and considered less authoritative than the more influential and editorially embellished Babylonian Talmud.

Yizkor (Hebrew: "Remember") Refers here to the prayer recited in the synagogue four times a year, during the holidays, on behalf of the dead: "May God remember the souls of the dead . . ."

Yoma A tractate of the Mishnah's second order, *Moed* ("Set Feasts"), which deals principally with the Day of Atonement.

Zevachim (Hebrew, "sacrifices") The name of a Talmudic tractate of the fifth order, *Kodashim* ("Hallowed Things"). The tractate deals with animal offerings.

ACKNOWLEDGMENTS

Many people contributed to the completion of this book. Those who listened while I read selected sections of the book and those who read sections aloud so that I could hear as well as read are too numerous to be individually mentioned. However, I would be amiss if I did not single out the following: first and foremost, my editor at Farrar, Straus and Giroux, Elisheva Urbas, whose perspicacity and insight, intuitive grasp of the material and feeling for language made me readily defer to her judgment; my colleagues Menachem Schmeltzer, Susan E. Shapiro, and Michael Brown, who read and commented on certain segments of the book and made substantial improvements; Gitelle Rapoport, who skillfully transcribed and edited early parts of the manuscript; and my student assistant Jonah Steinberg, who not only bore the brunt of the technical work associated with the preparation of a modern manuscript but also made valuable suggestions of style and content; and finally, my dear wife, Tzipora, who with

ACKNOWLEDGMENTS

her vast knowledge of the Holocaust not only contributed to, but also "lived" with me, the making of this book. It is better because of them.